PUGLIA
TRAVEL
G U I D E

Ultimate Travel Companion to

Experience The Puglia.

MATT HOOD
TRAVEL & TOUR

WELCOME TO

PUGLIA

Welcome to the undiscovered gem of Italy's heel—Puglia, a region that has blossomed from obscurity into the radiant star of the south.

Thankful to you for consenting to protected innovation guidelines by downloading this book through genuine methods and by not replicating, checking, or spreading any piece of this book.

Scan For Puglia Map

About Author

 Matt Hood is an established travel guidebook author, with more than 10 years of experience in the travel industry. A passionate traveller, Matt has travelled to over 30 countries and has written extensively about his experiences.

In addition to his travel guidebooks, Matt also contributes to numerous travel blogs and magazines. He holds a degree in travel and tourism from the University of Michigan and currently resides in San Francisco, California.

Matt Hood is the perfect guide for anyone looking to explore the world. Through his books, he provides readers with an insider's view of the places he visits and the people he meets, giving them the confidence and knowledge to make the most of their travels.

HOW TO USE THIS GUIDE

Welcome to your comprehensive guide to the captivating city of Puglia! To make the most of your travel experience, this guide is thoughtfully organized into chapters that cover various aspects of Puglia, ensuring you have all the essential information at your fingertips. Here's a breakdown of the contents and how to navigate through them:

CHAPTER 1: OVERVIEW OF PUGLIA

Delve into the essence of Puglia through its rich historical backdrop, cultural intricacies, and geographical tapestry. Uncover the evolution of this captivating region in history, its diverse culture, and the fascinating landscapes that define its topography.

CHAPTER 2: TRAVEL SMART

Equip yourself with essential insights to make your Puglia adventure seamless. Discover critical information on reaching Puglia and navigating within the region, along with optimal weather insights to ensure you experience Puglia at its finest.

CHAPTER 3: THE PUGLIA'S TOP 10

Explore the region's unmissable attractions, from the Gargano Peninsula's coastal allure to the historic marvel of Castel del Monte and the enchanting Trulli di Alberobello. Immerse yourself in the allure of destinations like Trani, Martina Franca, Ostuni, and more.

CHAPTER 4: THINGS TO DO IN PUGLIA

Tailor your experience with a plethora of activities - from beach escapades and invigorating boat trips to cycling adventures, shopping excursions, and vibrant nights out. Engage in hiking, horse riding, and delightful activities for the younger explorers.

CHAPTER 5: 5-DAY ITINERARIES IN PUGLIA

Embark on curated journeys through Puglia's diverse landscapes and cultural hubs. Traverse Trulli-laden delights, coastal wonders, baroque marvels, and urban explorations in specially crafted 5-day itineraries.

CHAPTER 6: EXPLORING PUGLIA

Uncover the essence of Bari, Lecce, and critical regions like the Gargano Peninsula, Gallipoli, and Valle d'Itria. Navigate through each destination, explore top attractions, and relish in specially designed 5-day trips.

CHAPTER 7: LOCAL CUISINES & DRINKS

Delight in the flavors of Puglia with its exquisite local cuisines and iconic drinks. Dive into regional specialties like Orecchiette con Cime di Rape, Taralli, and savor the region's culinary richness.

CHAPTER 8: WHERE TO EAT

Discover culinary gems across Puglia's diverse regions. Find the best dining spots in the Gargano Peninsula, Puglia Imperiale, Bari, Valle d'Itria, Salento, and Basilicata.

CHAPTER 9: WHERE TO STAY

Choose from a range of accommodation options across Bari, Gargano, Valle d'Itria, and Salento. Find your ideal stay amidst the region's captivating landscapes.

CHAPTER 10: USER FULL RESOURCES & CONTACTS

Access practical resources, including must-visit festivals, local phrases, tourist information centers, and emergency contacts to enhance your travel experience and ensure a hassle-free stay in Puglia.

TABLE OF CONTENTS

WELCOME TO PUGLIA

Welcome to the undiscovered gem of Italy's heel—Puglia, a region that has blossomed from obscurity into the radiant star of the south. I'm Matt Hood, and for two decades, Puglia has been both my muse and my playground. The northern Italians, considering it part of the Mezzogiorno, often overlooked its cultural offerings compared to the north. Yet, today presents a different story—Puglia shines as the newfound gem of the southern region.

When I first set foot in Puglia, it was a hidden treasure, largely untouched by foreign travelers. Northern Italians viewed it as a distant land, overshadowed by the cultural opulence of the north. But over the years, I've witnessed its transformation into a coveted destination. From the Foresta Umbra's lush greenery to the Valle d'Istria's enchanting white towns, each corner of Puglia unveils a unique story waiting to be explored.

My experiences in Puglia have been woven into the pages of this comprehensive travel guide. This book is not merely a collection of attractions and accommodations but a narrative that delves into the essence of Puglia—the rhythms of life, the flavors of its cuisine, and the allure of its landscapes. It's a meticulously detailed guidebook designed to be your companion as you traverse through this land of contrasts.

Puglia, aptly named the 'land of the two seas,' boasts Italy's longest coastline, where the Ionian and Adriatic Seas embrace its shores. From the dramatic cliffs of the Gargano peninsula to the sprawling plains of wheat fields and vineyards, this region offers a tapestry of natural beauty. The Trulli, those captivating cone-shaped dwellings dotting the countryside, stand as a testament to centuries of history. At the same time, the Valle d'Istria's white towns perch atop hills, inviting you to wander through their whitewashed alleys.

But beyond its picturesque landscapes, Puglia is a treasure trove of history. Greek and Roman remnants whisper tales of ancient civilizations. From the ruins in Taranto to the Greek-rooted villages in Salento, the echoes of a rich past resonate in every cobblestone street and old structure.

In the heart of Puglia, the trullo stands as an iconic symbol, each one a piece of living history. Alborebello was designated a UNESCO World Heritage site, boasting over a thousand of these charming structures. Amidst these architectural wonders lies the masserie, once fortified farms now transformed into stylish retreats, offering a glimpse into the region's rustic elegance.

Puglia has often been likened to Tuscany, yet it holds its unique allure. It's a place where time slows down, where the simplicity of rural life intertwines seamlessly with moments of indulgence. Unlike the manicured hills of Tuscany, Puglia's landscape is raw, its pace unhurried, inviting you to savor the art of idleness.

While Puglia has drawn the attention of celebrities and discerning travelers seeking authenticity, it remains untouched by the glossy veneer of commercialization. Its authenticity lies in its simplicity, in the humble family-run tavernas, and in the pristine stretches of coastline.

In these pages, I invite you to embrace Puglia in its purest form—a land of contrasts, where history whispers through ancient stones, where nature captivates with its diverse landscapes, and where the warmth of its people leaves an indelible mark on your soul. This guidebook is your key to unlocking the secrets and treasures of Puglia, a journey that promises both adventure and tranquility in equal measure.

CHAPTER 1

OVERVIEW

History Puglia

Culture Of Puglia

Geography & Topography Of Puglia

CHAPTER 1

OVERVIEW OF PUGLIA

History Puglia

The story of Puglia spans millennia, unfolding through epochs of triumph, conflict, and cultural fusion. Puglia's history, from the ancient remains of Altamura Man, found in Grotta di Lamalunga, to its present-day journey, is a vivid tapestry spun with tales of conquests, invasions, and unwavering resilience.

The region's early history reveals a flourishing relationship between the

Greeks and southern Italy, establishing trade links that culminated in Greek colonies in Magna Graecia. Taras, founded by exiles from Sparta, stood as the epitome of Greek prosperity, now remembered through remnants like the Doric Temple's surviving columns in Taranto.

However, as the Romans expanded southward, Puglia fell under their dominion, becoming a vital trade hub with the eastern Mediterranean.

Roman imprints endure today in scattered ruins like the Appian Way's columns in Brindisi and the grand amphitheater and theater in Lecce.

The region faced turbulent times following the fall of the Roman Empire, enduring invasions by barbarians and subsequent clashes between Byzantine forces and Lombard invaders. The Saracens, comprising Arabs, Spanish Muslims, and Berbers, furthered the region's turmoil, leading to their short-lived emirates in Bari and Taranto.

The Byzantine Empire's successful reconquest introduced waves of Greek settlers, embedding a significant Greek cultural influence in Puglia by the 10th and 11th centuries. However, the Norman arrival, initially as pilgrims visiting Christian shrines, transitioned into a Papal-supported military invasion that ousted the Byzantines.

Under the Hauteville dynasty, Puglia witnessed significant shifts, culminating in Roger II's coronation as the first king of Sicily. Norman rule left an indelible mark with architectural marvels, such as castles, cathedrals, and monuments, transforming port cities into bustling trade hubs during the Crusades.

Subsequent centuries saw Puglia's control oscillate between ruling dynasties—from the Angevins to the Spanish House of Aragon. Spanish rule marked an era of economic decline, corrupt governance, and exploitation of the populace.

The region's fate changed hands multiple times—ceding to the Austrian Habsburgs under the Treaty of Utrecht, then later returning to the Bourbon dynasty's rule. Napoleon's brief occupation ushered in reforms, but it was the Risorgimento movement and Garibaldi's 'Thousand' that marked a pivotal moment, integrating Puglia into the Kingdom of Italy in 1861.

Post-unification hardships, including increased taxes and economic decline, fueled mass emigration to the Americas in the late 19th century. Yet, in the aftermath of World War I, Puglia experienced stability, overcoming the malaria crisis and initiating agricultural reforms.

The region's industrial growth burgeoned in the mid-20th century, paralleled by internal migration to the north. Today, Puglia remains agriculturally robust, renowned for its olive oil and wine production, yet grappling with youth unemployment and contemporary migration challenges.

Puglia's tourism witnessed a surge, buoying its economy, until the COVID-19 pandemic brought a stark decline in visitors, echoing the global impact on tourism. Despite this setback, hopes are high for Puglia's economic recovery, especially with the EU's financial support aimed at rejuvenating the region post-pandemic.

Culture Of Puglia

The Culture of Apulia, known as Puglia in Italian, is a diverse mosaic crafted from its ancient past, varied influences, and lively customs.

Situated at the southeast tip of the Italian peninsula, Puglia has long been a crossroads where Western and Eastern cultures converge. Its strategic location on the coast of the Adriatic and Ionian seas has made it a historical bridge between Western Europe and the Balkans/Greece, creating a unique blend of influences.

The Jatta National Archaeological Museum, housed in the historic Jatta Palace in Ruvo di Puglia, stands as a testament to Puglia's rich past. The museum, an extraordinary 19th-century private collection, has remained unchanged since its inception. Collected by the judge and archaeologist Giovanni Jatta and his brother Giulio, the artifacts, especially ceramics from Magna Graecia, offer a glimpse into the region's ancient connections with Greece.

Another significant archaeological institution is the National Archaeological Museum of Taranto (MArTA), founded in 1887. It showcases artifacts spanning from the Paleolithic to the early Middle Ages, highlighting the history of Taranto and other regions in Apulia. Notable exhibits include the "Golds of Taranto," a collection of intricate gold jewelry pieces reflecting the region's expertise in metalwork during the 4th to 1st centuries B.C.

Apulian cuisine is a celebration of diversity, with recipes and ingredients varying by season. The culinary landscape features an array of vegetables, seafood, and meats. Orecchiette, a distinctive ear-shaped pasta, is a local favorite, often enjoyed with meat stew or rapini. Seafood dishes like cavatelli with mussels and grilled octopus showcase the region's coastal bounty.

The region boasts several products with Protected Designation of Origin (PDO), such as olive oils like Dauno and Terra di Bari, cheeses like caciocavallo silano, and wines with DOC, DOCG, and IGT designations. The emphasis on local, high-quality ingredients contributes to the uniqueness of Apulian gastronomy.

Puglia's traditions and folklore are deeply rooted in religious and cultural events. La Fòcara, a festival in Novoli, involves a massive bonfire illuminated by fireworks, commemorating the local patron saint, Anthony the Great. Tavole di San Giuseppe, celebrated in various towns, features large tables with typical dishes in honor of Saint Joseph.

The Holy Week is marked by solemn processions in Molfetta, Taranto, Francavilla Fontana, and other towns, each with its unique rituals and traditions. The Processione delle Fracchie in Lamis, featuring walking bonfires, is a striking spectacle.

Other festivities include the Palio di Taranto, a rowing competition reflecting the maritime heritage, and the Festa del Soccorso in San Severo, characterized by processions, fireworks, and a race alongside exploding fireworks.

The cultural richness of Puglia is further exemplified by events like the Torneo dei Rioni in Oria, a medieval festival with parades and traditional games, and the Pizzica Scherma de Torrepaduli, a dance in honor of Saint Roch featuring simulated fencing duels.

Geography & Topography Of Puglia

Puglia, situated in the southeastern region of Italy, showcases a variety of landscapes and distinctive geographical characteristics. Surrounded by the Adriatic and Ionian seas, it flaunts Italy's lengthiest coastline among its mainland regions. To the north, the Gargano promontory stretches into the Adriatic, resembling a "sperone" or spur, while the southern Salento peninsula forms Italy's boot-shaped "tacco" or heel.

The region showcases diverse topography. The Daunian Mountains, housing Monte Cornacchia, the highest peak at 1,152 meters (3,780 feet) above sea level, dominate the landscape. However, beyond the Alta Murgia National Park and Gargano National Park, Puglia generally features a flat terrain. Gentle undulations and moderate hills adorn the northern and western areas, contrasting with the notably more balanced Salento peninsula in the south.

Puglia experiences a predominantly Mediterranean climate characterized by scorching, dry summers and mild, rainy winters. Snowfall is rare, especially along the coast, though sporadic instances have occurred in recent years. Summers can be exceedingly hot and arid, with temperatures occasionally surpassing 40°C (104°F) in cities like Lecce and Foggia.

The coastal regions, particularly along the Adriatic and southern Salento,

face varied winds that significantly influence local weather. The Northerly Bora wind from the Adriatic Sea brings cooler temperatures and reduced humidity, providing relief from summer heat. Conversely, the Southerly Sirocco wind from North Africa raises temperatures and moisture, occasionally carrying red dust from the Sahara Desert. This fluctuation in wind patterns creates diverse conditions across different coastal towns on the same day.

The stretch from Otranto to Santa Maria di Leuca is a segment of the Regional Natural Coastal Park known as "Costa Otranto — Santa Maria di Leuca e Bosco di Tricase," designated by the Apulia Region in 2008.

This area boasts abundant natural marvels and historic landmarks, such as the rocky inlet of Ciolo.

Historically, Puglia witnessed significant emigration from economically challenged areas to northern Italy and other parts of Europe between 1956 and 1971. However, economic improvements led to a decline in this trend, with a period of net immigration between 1982 and 1985. Subsequent stagnation in employment conditions resulted in a renewed decrease in immigration since 1986.

CHAPTER 2

TRAVEL SMART

What You Need To Know

Getting to the Puglia

Getting Around Puglia

Weather and Best Time to Visit

MATT HOOD
TRAVEL & TOUR

CHAPTER 2

TRAVEL SMART

What You Need To Know

Currency: The official currency in Italy is the euro (€), divided into 100 cents. Coins come in denominations of 2, 5, 10, 20, and 50 cents, as well as 1 and 2 euros. Banknotes are available in 5, 10, 20, 50, 100, 200, and 500 euros.

Currency Exchange: Exchange currency at exchange offices (cambios), some banks, or post offices. Exchange offices often have longer hours, while banks and post offices might offer better rates.

Credit Cards: Visa and MasterCard are widely accepted. American Express might not be accepted everywhere. Major establishments, shops, hotels, restaurants, and petrol stations usually accept credit cards, but smaller places might prefer cash.

Opening Hours: Museums, galleries, churches, and castles have varying opening hours and might be closed on different days of the week. Banks operate from Monday to Friday, typically from 8:30 am to 1 pm, and then reopen from 2:30/3 pm to 4/4:30 pm. Shops generally open from Monday to Saturday, with some non-food shops closing on Mondays.

Public Holidays: Holidays such as New Year's Day (Capodanno), Easter Sunday and Monday (Pasqua e Pasquetta), Labour Day (Festa del Lavoro), and Christmas Day (Natale), among others, see closures in banks and most shops. Expect closures on these days and plan accordingly.

Safety and Security: Exercise caution against pickpockets, especially in crowded areas like ports and markets. Keep passports, valuable documents, and excess cash in a hotel safe. Be wary of Vespa-riding thieves and avoid leaving valuables in parked cars. In case of robbery, report it to local authorities promptly.

Emergency Numbers: In case of emergencies, dial 113 for general emergencies, 112 for police, 115 for fire, and 118 for an ambulance. For road assistance, call 116.

Language: English is spoken in main towns and tourist spots, but outside these areas, Italian is predominantly spoken. Puglia has its dialects, with Griko, a Greek dialect, being notable.

Healthcare: Healthcare services are generally good. The European Health Insurance Card (EHIC) might offer coverage, but travel insurance is advisable. For COVID-19, access to many museums requires proof of vaccination, recovery, or a recent negative test.

Electricity: Italy uses 220V/50Hz as standard. Visitors from other countries might require an adapter, while those from North America might need a transformer. The sockets are typically two- or three-round pins.

Time Zone: Italy is one hour ahead of Greenwich Mean Time (GMT). During daylight saving time, clocks move forward by an hour from the last Sunday in March to the last Sunday in October.

Religion: Puglia, like the rest of Italy, is predominantly Roman Catholic. Modest dress is expected when visiting places of worship, and religious festivals are integral to the local culture.

Telecommunications: To call an Italian number from outside Italy, use the international dialing code (+39) followed by the telephone number. Check with your mobile provider about roaming charges, or consider purchasing a local SIM card for extended stays.

Tipping: A service charge of 10–15% is often included in the bill. Extra tipping for exceptional service is appreciated. Tip porters, bar staff, and taxi drivers modestly as per custom.

Getting to the Puglia

Getting to Puglia offers various transportation options, mainly through air travel. The region is serviced by two major international airports: Karol Wojtyla Airport in Bari (IATA: BRI) and Brindisi Airport (IATA: BDS).

These airports serve as pivotal travel hubs, connecting Puglia to various European cities.

Karol Wojtyla Airport, Bari:

Situated 10 kilometers (6 miles) northwest of Bari city center, Karol Wojtyla Airport, also known as Palese Airport, provides a gateway to Puglia. Airlines like British Airways, Ryanair, and Easyjet offer regular flights from London Heathrow, London Stansted, and London Gatwick to Bari. The airport's website (www.aeroportidipuglia.it) provides essential information for travelers.

Transportation Options:

Shuttle Bus: Terravision, in partnership with Autoservizi Tempesta, operates a shuttle service to Bari's Central Station for €4 one way. The journey takes approximately 30 minutes and runs from 05:35 am to 12:10 am. Tickets are purchasable on the bus.

Public Bus: AMTAB Line 16 offers a budget-friendly option at €1 one way. Although slower due to frequent stops, tickets can be obtained from the newsagent inside the terminal.

Metropolitan Rail Service (F2 Line): The airport is connected to Bari Central Station by the F2 line, taking around 20 minutes. Tickets cost €5 one way and can be purchased online at www.ferrovienordbarese.it or the station.

Additionally, Pugliairbus (www.aeroportidipuglia.it) connects Bari Airport to other regional airports, such as Brindisi, Foggia, Taranto, and Matera in Basilicata.

Brindisi's Salento Airport:

Approximately 4 kilometers (2.5 miles) from Brindisi city center, Salento Airport primarily serves flights from Ryanair, connecting to UK cities like Stansted and Manchester. The airport's website (www.aeroportidipuglia.it) offers travel details and services.

Transportation Options:

- City Bus: A bus service operates every 30 minutes into Brindisi city center, taking roughly 30 minutes and costing €4.
- Direct Bus Service: There's an economical direct bus to Lecce as well.
- Taxi: Taxis to the city center are available for around €20 and take approximately 15 minutes.

These airports are key entry points to Puglia, providing essential travel connections for tourists and visitors alike. However, aside from air travel, the road network serves as a primary mode of transportation within the region. The A14 highway connects Bari to Taranto and further north along the Adriatic coast, while the A16 links Puglia to Naples in an east-west direction. The region is also expecting the completion of a high-speed rail line between Naples and Bari by 2027, aimed at enhancing travel accessibility within the area.

Getting Around Puglia

Buses in Puglia:

Puglia boasts a well-connected regional bus network operated by companies like SITA Sud, STP Bari, and Cotrap. While buses are generally more affordable than trains, reliability can vary due to traffic and schedules. For instance, a ticket from Bari to Alberobello typically costs around €5.

Car and Motorcycle Rentals:

Hiring a car or motorcycle is a popular and convenient way to explore Puglia, offering flexibility and accessibility to various destinations. Renowned companies like Avis, Budget, Europcar, Hertz, and Sixt provide car rental services in Puglia. Rental prices for small cars start at around £150 per week. Car rental companies usually require drivers to be 21–25 years old with a valid license and credit card. However, booking in advance and understanding local driving regulations, such as speed limits (130 km/h on motorways, 90 km/h on secondary roads, 50 km/h in towns), is advisable. Beware of potential issues like unclear signage, restricted traffic zones (ZTL), and parking challenges in historic centers.

Top Car Rental Companies:
- Avis: www.avis.com
- Budget: www.budget.com
- Europcar: www.europcar.com
- Hertz: www.hertz.com
- Sixt: www.sixt.com

Boat Tours:

Exploring Puglia's stunning coastal areas via boat tours is a popular choice for travelers. Rent Boat Puglia offers motorboat rentals starting from €290 per day. Websites like Getmyboat also provide options for boat rentals, with prices starting from $15 per hour. These rentals offer an opportunity to experience Puglia's coastal beauty and vibrant marine life.

Top Boat Rental Services:
- Rent Boat Puglia
- Getmyboat

Bicycles and Mopeds:

Cycle hire is readily available across towns and resorts in Puglia. Rental costs range from €15–20 per day and €35–€45 for three days. Electric bikes may be available for an additional fee. Puglia in Movimento offers a Bari bike service with free delivery to specified locations.

Top Bike Rental Services:

Puglia in Movimento (www.pugliainmovimento.com)

Taxi Services:

Taxis are easily accessible in Puglia, offering convenient travel options. Companies like EuroTaxi, Puglia VIP, and Taxi Apulia serve various areas, with fares determined by distance and travel time.

Public Transportation:

Puglia's public transportation system includes trains, facilitating travel between major cities and towns. The network is comprehensive, making it an efficient means to explore both popular and offbeat destinations.

Weather and Best Time to Visit

Puglia, nestled in the picturesque heel of Italy's boot, is blessed with a Mediterranean climate that shapes its distinctive weather patterns throughout the year. Understanding the climate conditions is crucial for planning an ideal visit, considering festivals and attractions that complement each season.

The Mediterranean climate of Puglia manifests in mild, relatively wet winters and hot, sunny summers, with occasional thunderstorms. The coastal areas experience a classic Mediterranean climate, with rainfall concentrated in autumn and winter. Bari, the capital situated on the coast, witnesses average temperatures ranging from 4.4°C in January to 30.5°C in August. Inland areas, such as the northern plain in Foggia, exhibit a slightly continental climate characterized by sweltering summers and cold nights in winter. The Salento peninsula, facing both the Adriatic and Ionian Seas, enjoys a mild yet windy environment.

Choosing the right time to visit Puglia is crucial for an optimal experience. Spring, early summer, and autumn emerge as the most favorable seasons. While July and August bring hot temperatures, reaching the mid-30s°C inland, they are also the busiest months with elevated prices due to high demand. May, June, and September offer pleasant temperatures in the 20s°C, ideal for activities like walking and cycling. April and October are also favorable, albeit with occasional rain and cooler days.

Winter:

Carnevale di Putignano: Puglia hosts the world's longest festival, Carnevale di Putignano, running from Boxing Day to Shrove Tuesday. This lively celebration is a vibrant showcase of local traditions and carnival revelry.

Spring:

Evening Festivals: Spring in Puglia is perfect for participating in evening festivals by the sea or strolling through historic centers nestled in the hills. The region comes alive with cultural events, providing a unique opportunity to immerse in local traditions.

Summer:

Beach Delights: Puglia's summer is a paradise for sun and sea lovers. The region boasts numerous white sandy beaches and rocky coasts, inviting visitors to bask in the Mediterranean sun and enjoy the crystal-clear waters.

Autumn:

Grape Harvesting: As autumn sets in, visitors can partake in the grape harvesting festivities, gaining insight into the winemaking process from its inception. This hands-on experience offers a glimpse into Puglia's rich agricultural traditions.

CHAPTER 3

THE PUGLIA'S TOP 10

The Gargano Peninsula

Castel del Monte

I Trulli di Alberobello

Trani

Grotte di Castellana

Martina Franca

Ostuni

Otranto

Matera

Vieste

MATT HOOD
TRAVEL & TOUR

CHAPTER 3

THE PUGLIA's TOP 10

The Gargano Peninsula

Nature's Serene Haven

Nestled in the northernmost part of Puglia, the Gargano Peninsula stands as an untouched paradise, with its rugged, untamed beauty offering a captivating escape. Jutting into the Adriatic, it forms the unmistakable "spur" of Italy's boot, boasting a unique blend of coastal wonders and lush hinterlands. Embraced by beguiling blue-green waters and lined with craggy limestone cliffs, the Gargano Peninsula entices travelers seeking a pristine retreat away from bustling tourist circuits.

A historical and geographical sub-region within the province of Foggia, the Gargano is a mountainous peninsula that embodies natural splendor. Its isolation and geographical disposition, surrounded by the Adriatic Sea on three sides, have earned it the moniker "the spur of Italy." This broad massif, comprising highlands and peaks, holds a captivating tale of evolution. Once an island distinct from the mainland, its union with the land has left an indelible mark on its fauna and flora, shaping its unique environment.

The Gargano Peninsula offers abundant experiences for enthusiastic adventurers. Its coastline features immaculate Adriatic beaches, enticing visitors to soak up the sun and relish the clear waters. The Foresta Umbra National Park, a verdant treasure trove, unfolds with hiking trails that wind through its thick foliage, offering glimpses of a serene wilderness. Medieval towns with charming historic centers dot the landscape, each narrating tales of bygone eras. Moreover, the Gargano houses significant religious pilgrimage sites, including Monte Sant'Angelo sul Gargano, home to the oldest shrine dedicated to the Archangel Michael in Western Europe.

Practical Information:
- Location: Province of Foggia, Puglia, Southeast Italy
- Accessibility: Accessible from Manfredónia, about a 2.5-hour drive from Bari airport
- Contact Information for Transportation: SITA (tel. 0881-773117) or ATAF (tel. 0881-724088)

- Highlights: Adriatic beaches, Foresta Umbra National Park, medieval towns, pilgrimage sites, and exquisite local cuisine

While reaching the Gargano may involve navigating slow roads, the journey rewards with an unparalleled landscape. From serene coastlines to dense forests, the Gargano Peninsula invites travelers to immerse themselves in its untouched allure, embracing nature's pristine bounty.

Castel del Monte

A Timeless Enigma

Perched majestically atop a 540-meter-high rocky peak, Castel del Monte stands as an enigmatic jewel of medieval architecture in Puglia. Emperor Frederick II's stronghold, this UNESCO World Heritage Site, captivates visitors with its unique octagonal design, drawing influence from both European and Middle Eastern architectural styles. Its purpose and design intricacies have long puzzled historians, adding an air of mystery to its grandeur.

Commissioned by King Frederick II in the 13th century, Castel del Monte reflects the erudition and cultural depth of its creator. Its construction, completed around 1240, showcases not only precise architectural geometry but also hints at a fascination with astronomy, leading to debates about its intended purpose—a defensive fortress or lavish royal residence. Despite lacking traditional fortress features, its sturdy walls and towers suggest strategic significance within Frederick's network of defensive castles.

Pratical Informations:

- Address: Federico II di Svevia Square, Andria, Bari, 701221
- Opening Hours: October 1st to March 31st - 9:00 am to 5:45 pm; April 1st to September 30th - 10:00 am to 6:45 pm
- Last Admission: October to March - 5:00 pm; April to September - 6:00 pm
- Full Price Ticket: €9.00; Reduced Price (18-25 years old EU citizens): €2.00
- Contact: +39 32798055512
- Official Website: www.casteldelmonte.beniculturali.it

The castle's interior, though sparse, echoes its grandeur from bygone eras. Though looted of its treasures, the chambers once adorned with mosaics, paintings, and tapestries transport visitors to an era of opulence. The lack of traditional fortress features piques curiosity, inviting guests to explore its architectural marvels and ponder its multifaceted history.

Nestled in Andria, Castel del Monte presides over the Murgia region's scenic landscape near the Adriatic Sea. Its distinct octagonal shape, mathematical precision, and cultural significance earned it UNESCO's recognition as a masterpiece of medieval military architecture in 1996.

Trulli di Alberobello

An Enchanting Heritage

Nestled in the picturesque southern Italian region of Puglia, Trulli di Alberobello stands as an extraordinary testament to ancient building techniques. These captivating limestone dwellings showcase the ingenious corbelled dry-stone construction, an architectural style dating back centuries, and a unique treasure of the Mediterranean.

Dating back to the mid-14th century, the trulli of Alberobello represent a historical gem characterized by their distinctive pyramidal, domed, or conical roofs crafted from meticulously placed limestone slabs. While rural trulli can be found scattered along the Itria Valley, Alberobello boasts the highest concentration and best-preserved examples of these architectural marvels. In the districts of Rione Monti and Aja Piccola, more than 1500 of these distinctive structures contribute to the town's allure.

Strolling through the streets of Alberobello's designated trulli quarters immerses visitors in a fairy-tale-like setting. The enchanting sight of these cylindrical structures with whitewashed walls and conical roofs, meticulously constructed without mortar, evokes a sense of wonder and fascination. While many trulli are private residences, some offer guided tours or house museums, offering glimpses into their unique architecture and historical significance.

As individual trulli might have varying accessibility or tours, it's advisable to contact local tourism offices or specific trullo accommodations for guided tours or further information.

Local Tourism Office: Contact the Alberobello Tourism Office for guidance on visiting trulli: https://www.visitalberobello.com/en/

Trani

A Gem by the Adriatic

- Address: Via Tenente Luigi Morrico, 2 - 76125 Trani, Italy
- City Hall Contact: +39 0883-581111

Situated by the glistening Adriatic Sea, Trani emerges as a captivating city known as the 'Pearl of Puglia.' Its historic significance, marked by the splendid Cattedrale di San Nicola Pellegrino, medieval monuments, and vibrant cultural spaces, invites travelers to delve into its rich heritage.

Trani's historical roots date back to Roman times and flourished during the Norman and Swabian reigns due to its strategic trade links with the Middle East. The city's maritime prominence led to the creation of one of the oldest naval law codes, Ordinamenta et consuetudo maris, in 1063.

Under Emperor Frederick II's rule in the 13th century, Trani reached the zenith of its prosperity, seen in the grandeur of its architecture and bustling port. Today, it stands as a testament to its rich past, offering a blend of historical allure and seaside beauty, inviting visitors to wander its marble streets and savor the vibrant culture and captivating views along the Adriatic coast.

Top Trani Attractions:

Cattedrale di San Nicola Pellegrino:

- Address: Piazza Duomo, Trani
- Opening Hours: April–Oct: Mon–Sat 9am–12.30 pm, 3.30–7 pm; Sun 9 am–12.30 pm, 4–8.30 pm. Nov–Mar: Closes at 6 pm, 8.30 pm on Sundays.
- Admission: Free entry; charge for campanile climb.

The cathedral, an exquisite example of Apulian-Romanesque architecture, houses splendid bronze doors and a lower church adorned with centuries-old frescoes. Climb 258 steps to the top of the Campanile for stunning views.

Castello Svevo:

- Address: Lungomare Colombo, Trani
- Opening Hours: Wed-Mon 8.30 am–7.30 pm
- Admission: Ticketed entry; museum with restoration finds.

Guarding the seashore, this Swabian Castle from the 13th century showcases Trani's medieval past, boasting square designs and imposing towers.

Jewish Quarter:

Explore narrow alleys to discover medieval churches, palaces, and remnants of Trani's rich Jewish history, including synagogues converted into churches.

Chiesa di Ognissanti:

- Address: Via Ognissanti, Trani
- Opening Hours: Mon-Sat 9 am-noon; Fri & Sat 4–8 pm
- Admission: Free entry.

This restored 12th-century church with Knights Templar connections offers a picturesque view of the charming port.

Grotte di Castellana

Unveiling Nature's Subterranean Majesty

Pratical Informations:

- Address: Grotte di Castellana Srl, Piazzale Anelli 70013, Castellana Grotte, Bari, Apulia, Italy
- Phone: +39 080 4998221
- Email: segreteria@grottedicastellana.it
- Website: https://www.grottedicastellana.it/
- Opening Hours & Admission:
  Open from Monday to Friday:
  Monday: 08:30 - 12:00
  Tuesday: 08:30 - 12:00 | 15:30 - 17:00
  Wednesday: 08:30 - 12:00
  Thursday: 08:30 - 12:00 | 15:30 - 17:00
  Friday: 08:30 - 12:00
- Admission Fees:
  Complete Itinerary: €18 (Reduced €15)
  Short Itinerary: €15 (Reduced €12)

Free for children up to 5 years; reduced price for children from 6 to 14 years.

Nestled approximately 1.5km from Castellana Grotte, the Grotte di Castellana beckons explorers to embark on a journey into its wondrous depths. This extensive underground wonderland is revered as one of Italy's most breathtaking and magnificent cave systems, enticing visitors with its awe-inspiring natural formations.

Spanning an impressive 3.348 meters and reaching depths of 122 meters below street level, the Grotte di Castellana unveils an ethereal world hidden beneath the surface. As visitors venture through this labyrinthine system, they encounter a mesmerizing array of stalactites, stalagmites, and intricate limestone formations. The caves, maintaining a constant temperature of around 16.5°C, offer a fascinating glimpse into the geological marvels sculpted over millions of years.

The history of these caves dates back to the upper Cretaceous period, around 100 to 90 million years ago, when Puglia was submerged beneath the ancient Mediterranean Sea. The unique landscape owes its creation to the erosive action of rainwater on limestone rocks, carving out these mesmerizing underground caverns. Discovered on January 23rd, 1938, by speleologist Franco Anelli, these caverns hold testament to nature's enduring artistic prowess, inviting curious adventurers to witness their captivating beauty firsthand.

Martina Franca

A Jewel of Baroque Grandeur

Pratical Information:

- Address: Piazza Roma, 35, 74015 Martina Franca, Italy
- Phone Number: +39 080 4836111
- Wednesday Market Hours: Commences around 6:00 or 7:00 a.m. and concludes by 1:00 p.m.
- Attraction Entry: Most attractions such as the Church of San Martino and the historic center offer free entry.

Nestled in the heart of the enchanting Valle d'Itria, Martina Franca stands as a captivating small town in Puglia, Italy's beguiling heel. It's an embodiment of southern Italian charm and elegance, exuding unique characteristics that distinguish it from the region's treasures.

Established in the 10th century by refugees fleeing the Arab invasion of

Taranto, Martina Franca was christened from the devotion to St. Martin. The moniker 'Franca' was bestowed in 1310, signifying the city's privileges. This town bore witness to historical feats, including its defense against besieging French troops in 1529 during the war against Emperor Charles V.

Martina Franca is celebrated for its Baroque magnificence, showcasing a vibrant history seen in its narrow streets, magnificent churches, and graceful 18th-century townhouses adorned with intricate wrought-iron balconies. The town radiates a vibrant aura, featuring chic shops and culinary delights accentuated by superb cold meats, cheeses, pasta, and its renowned local white wine, Martina Franca.

The charming Piazza XX Settembre, lined with trees, serves as the town's central square and a popular gathering spot for the passeggiata. Visitors are greeted by the grandeur of Palazzo Ducale, originally a 14th-century castle transformed into a 17th-century palace. The palace, now the town hall, offers glimpses into the royal apartments adorned with Murano glass chandeliers and rococo murals by Domenico Carella.

A stroll along Corso Vittorio Emanuele leads to the magnificent Chiesa di San Martino, adorned with a sculptural group depicting St. Martin and an opulent interior showcasing a profusion of colored marble. The charming squares and alleys unveil Martina Franca's architectural treasures, including the Palazzo dell'Università and lovely Baroque porticos sheltering local restaurants.

Ostuni

The Enchanting "White City"

Pratical Information:

- Address: Ostuni, Province of Brindisi, Apulia, Italy
- Coordinates: 40.733°N 17.583°E
- Shop Hours: Winter: 9:00 AM - 1:00 PM & 4:30 PM - 8:00 PM
- Summer: 9:00 AM - 1:00 PM & 5:00 PM - 9:30 PM

Perched majestically atop a hill, Ostuni, known as the "White City," beckons travelers to experience the allure of Southern Italy. Its historical center is a labyrinth of narrow, winding streets adorned with dazzling whitewashed houses, quaint shops, and inviting eateries, offering a glimpse into the charm and culture of the region.

Ostuni's roots date back to ancient times, with traces of habitation since the Stone Age. Initially established by the Messapii, it faced near-total destruction during the Punic Wars under Hannibal's assault, only to be resurrected by the Romans. Between 1300 and 1463, it belonged to the Principality of Taranto. Subsequently, it came under the rule of Isabella, Duchess of Bari, marking an era of prosperity during the Italian Renaissance.

Approximately 8 km inland from the coast, Ostuni captivates visitors with its timeless allure. The town's architectural splendor showcases a fascinating blend of historical influences, featuring splendid structures resonating with the legacies of ancient tribes, Romans, and Renaissance prosperity.

While the town itself is a masterpiece with its maze of streets and whitewashed facades, Ostuni offers additional experiences. Private tours of the Medieval Village via Tuk Tuk provide in-depth explorations of the town's historical tapestry, enabling visitors to delve into its rich past and witness its architectural marvels. Certain attractions have separate fees, e.g., private tours starting at $39.49 per adult.

Ostuni invites travelers to immerse themselves in its winding streets, discover hidden treasures, and savor the local pace of life. From its vibrant shops to charming eateries and historical landmarks, every corner exudes the distinct essence of this enchanting hilltop town.

Otranto

A Tapestry of History and Courage

Practical Information:
- Address: Piazza Castello, 73028 Otranto LE, Italy
- Cathedral of Otranto Hours: Open Sunday to Saturday from 7:00 AM to 12:00 PM and 3:00 PM to 5:00 PM

Nestled southeast of Lecce, Otranto stands as Italy's easternmost town, perched proudly on a rocky promontory gazing over the Adriatic shores toward Albania. This picturesque town, born from Greek origins, boasts a captivating history and a resilient spirit.

The defining moment in Otranto's history unfolded during the 1480 siege by an Ottoman fleet, etching an indelible mark of bravery. Despite facing overwhelming odds, the townspeople, unwavering in their faith, chose martyrdom over surrender. The brutal massacre of 800 locals who refused conversion to Islam led to their canonization as the Blessed Martyrs of Otranto in 2013.

Otranto's charm radiates from its historic quarter, adorned with seafront restaurants and idyllic white beaches, making it a coveted destination. Perched on a hill, the Aragonese Castle, constructed after the 1480 invasion, echoes the town's resilient spirit. The awe-inspiring Cattedrale dell'Annunziata, built by the Normans in the 11th century, unveils a mosaic-adorned floor depicting The Tree of Life and the Capella dei Martiri housing the bones of the slain martyrs.

Beyond its historical treasures, Otranto boasts sandy beaches stretching northwards, kissed by the azure sea and sheltered by pine forests. The Baia dei Turchi, a sought-after beach linked by shuttle bus, lures sun-seekers during peak seasons.

For the intrepid traveler, the drive to Santa Maria di Leuca, Italy's Land's End, unveils a rugged coastline punctuated by ruined watchtowers and breathtaking vistas. A journey through this dramatic landscape offers glimpses of Corfu and Albania's coastline on a clear day, a testament to the allure of this southern Italian gem.

Matera

An Enigmatic Time Capsule

- Practical Information:
- Address: Matera, Basilicata, Italy
- Phone: +39 (0)835.241340 – 2413842
- Email: info@materawelcome.it
- Website: https://www.materawelcome.it/
- Opening Hours & Admission: Churches typically open daily from 10 AM to 7 PM (Nov–March 10 AM–4 PM).

Tucked away in the region of Basilicata, bordering Puglia, lies Matera, a city steeped in an enigmatic history that transcends millennia.
This UNESCO World Heritage site, acknowledged as the European Capital of Culture in 2019, presents a unique view of cave dwellings,

underground churches, and a captivating story carved into its limestone terrain.

Matera's story weaves through the annals of time, stretching back to the Paleolithic era, marking it as one of the world's oldest continuously inhabited cities. Its compelling allure lies in the Sassi districts—districts showcasing homes carved into natural caves or fashioned from soft limestone, a practice that originated in prehistoric times. These underground dwellings, once deemed uninhabitable, now redefine luxury as some of Europe's most exotic cave hotels.

The city's heart beats within the Sassi, divided into the Sasso Barisano and the Sasso Caveoso—labyrinths of alleys, stone stairways, and hidden courtyards. Navigating these ancient lanes, whether guided or self-led, immerses travelers in an atmospheric journey through Matera's rich history. The rupestrian churches, carved by monks from the 9th to 15th centuries, house remarkable frescoes and stand as testaments to centuries-old craftsmanship.

Once labeled the "City of Shame," the Sassi were vacated in the 1950s due to squalid living conditions, only to witness a revival in the 1980s. UNESCO's designation of the Sassi as a World Heritage Site in 1993 catalyzed restoration efforts and bolstered tourism. Presently, Matera stands as a testament to human resilience, embracing its history while welcoming a future that resonates through its ancient streets.

Vieste

- Location: Vieste, Province of Foggia, Puglia, Italy
- Website: https://www.visitvieste.com/

Vieste often hailed as the "Pearl of the Gargano," sits majestically on the eastern edge of the Gargano promontory in Puglia, Italy. This enchanting seaside town is a harmonious blend of timeless allure and contemporary resort amenities, making it an ideal haven for those seeking exploration and relaxation in equal measure.

With origins tracing back to the 10th century BC, Vieste proudly wears the marks of history etched by multiple civilizations. The town has weathered invasions and hosted diverse rulers, including the Byzantines, Lombards, Romans, and Greeks. Established primarily by the Normans in the 11th century, Vieste stood as a stronghold under the Svevo (Swabian) emperor Frederick II. Its storied past includes reigns under the Angevins and Aragonese, weaving a tapestry of historical significance and cultural diversity.

Vieste offers a tapestry of experiences, where the winding streets of the old town beckon exploration, while the captivating coastline invites leisurely beachside respites. Visitors can immerse themselves in the free-to-explore parts of the town, including the charming old quarter and picturesque beaches. Additionally, various activities, such as boat tours along the coastline, promise captivating experiences, albeit with associated fees.

Explorers eager to discover Vieste can plan their visits knowing that most restaurants take a midday hiatus, closing around 2:30 PM and reopening in the evening for dinner between 6 and 7 PM. For more detailed information and planning, the official Visit Vieste website serves as a valuable resource. Most parts of the town, including the old village and beaches, are free to explore. However, certain activities like boat tours may require fees. For instance, a group cruise along the coastline by Tour Desiree costs approximately €253.

CHAPTER 4

THINGS TO DO IN PUGLIA

CHAPTER 4

THINGS TO DO IN PUGLIA

Beaches & Boat Trips

Puglia unfolds an impressive 800km of coastline, offering diverse landscapes from pristine beaches to rocky terrains. While some areas boast white sands and splendid resorts, others showcase dry terrain and underwhelming beachfront. The Gargano Peninsula and Salento stand out for their best beaches. It's wise to avoid the peak season from mid-July through August due to crowded beaches with Italian holidaymakers. Several beaches charge an access fee, especially at exclusive beach clubs in Salento that offer upscale amenities at higher prices.

Puglia's captivating coastline invites a plethora of outdoor pursuits, from unwinding on beaches to embarking on thrilling boat trips. Resorts offer boat or yacht excursions to explore coastal caves, striking rock formations, and perhaps even spot dolphins. For an independent adventure, renting jet skis, dinghies, or motorboats is an option.

Top Beaches in Puglia:

- Baia dei Turchi: Historical significance marks this spot, where Turkish pirates landed five centuries ago.

- Bahia Porto Cesareo: Known for its beautiful waters and exceptional service.

- Togo Bay Beach: Offers high-quality amenities and delightful culinary options.

- Spiaggia di Punta Prosciutto: A lengthy expanse of soft dunes meeting the Ionian Sea's azure waters.

- Torre Lapillo: Features soft white sands and turquoise waters, offering a delightful beach experience.

- Sant'Andrea's Stacks: Famous for remarkable stacks emerging from the deep blue sea.

Boat Trips in Puglia:

- Boat trip to the Polignano a Mare caves: Modern boat rentals for excursions along the picturesque coast between Polignano and Monopoli.
- Guided Tour by Catamaran with Aperitif from Polignano a Mare: A sailing catamaran tour offering a splendid view of Polignano a Mare's historic centre and caves.
- Desirèe Experience. Visit the marine caves of Vieste: A boat tour to discover the enchanting Gargano coast.
- Rentme Boat Party: Renting crewed sailing and motor boats for daily trips along the coastline from Polignano to Monopoli.
- Noleggio Barche Durlindana: Offers various services, from pedal boats to guided cave tours in the area.

Cycling

Cycling is a popular outdoor activity in **Puglia,** offering a unique way to explore the region's stunning landscapes, historical sites, and charming villages. It's advisable to avoid the intense heat and increased traffic in July and August, making spring or autumn the ideal times for a cycling holiday.

The Gargano Peninsula in the north presents a challenging yet rewarding terrain for cyclists with its mountainous landscape. Further south along the flat coastland and gently undulating interior, cycling becomes more accessible. The Itria Valley Salentine cities of Lecce, Gallipoli, and Otranto also offer favourable cycling routes.

Many hotels provide bikes for guest use, and rentals are readily available in most towns and resorts. Tourist offices often have cycle maps with recommended routes. Online resources like www.pisteciclabili.com, specifically the Apulia section, offer maps of cycle paths and itineraries.

For those seeking guided or self-guided cycling holidays, various companies specialize in tours ranging from half a day to a week or more. These tours typically include accommodation, breakfast, luggage transport, GPS devices with programmed routes, detailed maps, route notes, 24-hour assistance, and insurance.

Noteworthy cycling routes in Puglia include:
- A Bike Ride Painted Blue: A leisurely 136 km ride along the coast from Bari to Brindisi, passing through trulli, country vegetable gardens, and bays with crystal-clear waters.
- Salento: Sun, Sea, and Wind: A 186 km route from the hinterland to the sea, traversing Salento's villages, Mediterranean scrub, and olive tree-lined landscapes.
- From the Sea into the Countryside: A 100 km route through rural landscapes featuring blooming nature, cherry and almond trees.
- Mountain Bike in the Umbra Forest: A moderate 55 km MTB & E-MTB route.
- The Magic of the Valle d'Itria: An easy/moderate 55 km Bike touring and e-bike route.
- A Balcony Overlooking the Apulian Sea: An easy/moderate 52 km Bike touring & E-Bike route.

Several reputable companies offering biking tours in Puglia include 4Cycling' n Trek (www.4cyclingandtrek.com/en), Ciclovagando (www.ciclovagando.com), and Puglia Cycle Tours (www.pugliacycletours.com).

Shopping

Shopping in Puglia is an immersive experience, showcasing a variety of local products and specialities that reflect the region's rich culture and history. From bustling markets to high-end boutiques, the shopping scene offers something for everyone, including delectable gastronomic delights and unique artisanal crafts.

Puglia's shopping scene isn't limited to these districts; it extends to numerous local shops, markets, and delicatessens across towns. The region is celebrated for its culinary delights, and visitors can explore bustling markets offering fresh fruits, vegetables, seafood, meats, and the iconic local pasta known as orecchiette. Additionally, notable specialities include olive oil, cured meats, cheeses, and the traditional papier-mâché crafted in Lecce, where visitors can even participate in cartapesta classes to learn this ancient craft. For the avid shopper, Puglia's shopping districts provide a glimpse into the region's diverse offerings, from local arts to contemporary goods.

Top Shopping Districts in Puglia
- Polignano a Mare: Renowned for speciality and gift shops, offering a delightful combination of beauty, nature, history, architecture, people, and food.
- Mercato di Vieste: A flea market situated at the bottom end of the main street, featuring local produce and handmade crafts.

- Puglia Village: A factory outlet providing a great shopping experience with branded clothing and accessories at discounted prices.
- Parco Commerciale di Casamassima: Positioned around Bari, this hub is ideal for various goods, including clothing, electronics, and groceries.
- Fashion Centre of Puglia: Located in Bari, known for textiles, furniture, wooden artefacts, and footwear.
- Barimax Shopping Village: This mall features clothing, accessories, and home goods.

Unique Things to Shop in Each District
- Polignano a Mare: Local crafts, souvenirs, and delightful food items.
- Mercato di Vieste: Offers an array of local produce and unique handmade crafts.
- Puglia Village: Branded clothing and accessories are available at discounted rates.
- Parco Commerciale di Casamassima: A diverse selection of goods encompassing clothing, electronics, and groceries.
- Centro Commerciale GrandApulia: Various products ranging from fashion to home goods.
- Fashion Centre of Puglia: Known for textiles, furniture, wooden artefacts, and footwear.
- Barimax Shopping Village: Features clothing, accessories, and items for the home.

Entertainments & Night Life

Puglia, the captivating heel of Italy's boot, boasts a diverse entertainment scene catering to a wide array of tastes. From cultural performances to vibrant nightlife and outdoor activities, the region offers a plethora of options for every visitor.

Puglia is home to several theatres that showcase a variety of performances, including theatre, opera, revue, ballet, puppet shows, and musicals. Both Bari and Lecce enjoy a cultural program that includes ballet, opera, and classical music. The Teatro Petruzzelli in Bari, a splendid venue, stands as the fourth-largest theatre in Italy, hosting local and international productions.

Concert enthusiasts will find Puglia to be a haven for musical diversity. Classical concerts, pop music performances, and jazz concerts grace the stages of various venues across the region. Puglia comes alive after sunset with a vibrant nightlife scene. Bari, a university city, offers lively bars, discos, and eateries, particularly around Piazza Mercantile in Old Bari. Notable spots include Cotriero, for its relaxed ambience and live music, and Gallery Pub, a popular venue for drinks. Wine enthusiasts can explore wine bars like Vino & Amore.

For those who prefer outdoor pursuits, Puglia offers a diverse range of activities. From bus tours and nature excursions to beach and pool clubs, the region provides options for all preferences. Visitors can engage in wildlife tours, geologic explorations, private sightseeing tours, walking tours, and even culinary experiences.

Salento emerged as a popular nightlife destination, particularly in summer. Gallipoli attracts hundreds of young people with its cocktail bars, beach parties, and open-air discos. Samsara Beach in Baia Verde is renowned for its vibrant nightlife, drawing crowds for non-stop dancing. Other lively spots include Porto Cesareo, Santa Maria di Leuca, Castro, Santa Terme Cesarea, and Castro.

The Salento region hosts a rich calendar of festivals and events, transforming city squares and streets into lively hubs at night. This cultural vibrancy adds an extra layer to the nightlife experience. Lecce, a university city, boasts an excellent selection of restaurants and watering holes. From rustic bars to trendy establishments with craft beers and exotic cocktails, Lecce caters to diverse tastes. The Teatro Politeama Greco in Lecce hosts a variety of shows and concerts, while the annual Festival del Cinema Europeo in April showcases the latest European film releases.

Hiking

Begin an unforgettable journey delving into Puglia's varied terrains via its expansive web of hiking paths. Traverse from the verdant woodlands of the Gargano Peninsula to the time-honoured trails of shepherds and the rugged Salento coastline. Puglia opens its doors to hiking aficionados, inviting them to deeply engage with the area's breathtaking landscapes and storied past.

Hiking in Puglia unveils a unique perspective on the region, renowned for its breathtaking landscapes, historic sites, and picturesque villages. As you traverse the trails, you'll encounter dazzling whitewashed towns, iconic trulli with their distinctive conical roofs, and ancient olive groves. The historical significance of the architecture and the endless coastline add to the allure of Puglia's hiking experience.

Spring and autumn stand as perfect seasons for exploring Puglia by foot, offering hikers pleasant weather and vibrant scenery. The Valle d'Itria, with its rolling hills adorned by olive groves and vineyards, emerges as a renowned region for week-long hiking escapades.

Popular Hiking Routes:
Bosco delle Pianelle: Explore one of the last great forests in Puglia, offering a plethora of marked trails for an immersive hiking experience.

Il Sentiero Vecchio del Ciolo: Enjoy a scenic trail with opportunities to pause and admire panoramic views of the sea, observe swimmers below and discover hidden caves.

Parco delle Querce: Immerse yourself in the beauty of a park surrounded by dry stone walls perched high above the sea, providing a stunning backdrop for your hiking adventure.

Via del Sale Ionica: Traverse a captivating hiking trail, experiencing the natural beauty and diverse landscapes that Puglia has to offer.

Via Peuceta - Cammino Materano: Embark on a historic trail that promises a blend of nature and cultural exploration, showcasing the region's diverse heritage.

Gole di Accadia: Discover one of the most intriguing rocky environments in the Gargano area, offering a unique hiking experience surrounded by natural wonders.

Monte Nero: Conquer a mountainous hiking trail that promises both challenges and breathtaking vistas, providing a memorable adventure for hikers.

Valle dell'Inferno: Explore a trail that winds through the picturesque Valle dell'Inferno, offering hikers a captivating journey through the region's diverse landscapes.

Sentiero di Fajarama: Embark on a hiking trail that unfolds the beauty of Puglia, revealing hidden gems and allowing hikers to connect with the region's natural splendour.

Sentiero Forestale Pila del Ladro: Traverse a scenic hiking trail that winds through captivating landscapes, providing hikers with an opportunity to immerse themselves in Puglia's natural wonders.

Horse Riding

Exploring Puglia on horseback offers a unique perspective on the region's breathtaking landscapes and coastal beauty. In Puglia, there are various riding experiences suitable for both seasoned riders and beginners.

Critical destinations for horse riding adventures in Puglia include:
Parco Naturale Regionale Costa Otranto – Santa Maria di Leuca e Bosco di Tricase: This natural park is a haven for riders, boasting forests, rolling hills, and a stunning coastline that caters to various riding terrains.

Centro Equestre Parco di Mare: Situated near Cisternino, this centre provides horse riding lessons and excursions, offering gentle rides through olive groves or more challenging routes along the coastline.

Beyond picturesque scenery, horse riding in Puglia offers a cultural immersion into local traditions and heritage. Many stables and schools provide insights into the region's history and cuisine, often including meals and wine tastings as part of the riding experiences.

Children Activities

In Puglia, families with children have plenty of activities and attractions to explore together. While there aren't many kid-specific spots, the region's sandy, gently sloping beaches—many awarded blue flags—are great for families. However, keep an eye on rough sea conditions marked by warning flags. Children often enjoy exploring rocky coves, and older kids with good swimming skills might find fun in jumping off lower rocks, especially in places like Polignano al Mare, famous for the Red Bull Cliff Diving event.

A day trip to the Tremiti islands offers boat excursions to caves and crystal-clear waters, perfect for snorkelling, which can be a hit with older children. Exploring castles across the region can also be an exciting adventure for kids. Families can stay in unique hobbit-style trulli or holiday farms (agriturismo) where kids can engage in outdoor activities like cherry picking or countryside exploration via horseback, bike rides, or walks.

The primary attraction aimed at children in Puglia is the Zoo Safari near Fasano. It's a sizeable animal-themed park where visitors can drive through safari-style (using their cars) and encounter giraffes and other animals. Expect crowds, particularly in summer. Nearby Fasanolandia, under the same management, features amusement rides and water slides but is less popular than Zoo Safari.

Here are some family-friendly activities and attractions in Puglia:
- I Trulli di Alberobello - World Heritage Site: Alberobello's Trulli houses with conical roofs are a delight for kids.
- Grotte di Castellana: An underground cave system offering an adventurous exploration for children.
- Zoo safari Fasanolandia: One of Europe's largest safari parks near Fasano, providing an immersive wildlife experience.
- Beaches: Puglia's sandy beaches, many with beach clubs offering games and kid-friendly equipment, are perfect for family fun.
- Boat Tour with Dolphin Observation: Explore the northern Ionian Sea and observe cetaceans with a scientific research association.
- Castello Aragonese: Discover Taranto's history at this fascinating castle.
- Basilica San Nicola: A magnificent cathedral in Bari's old town.
- Centro Storico, Lecce: Lecce's historic city centre is a must-visit, offering beautiful sights and experiences.
- Centro Storico di Polignano a Mare: The charming alleys and waterfront make for an awe-inspiring walk.
- Centro Storico Otranto: Explore historical buildings and captivating shops in Otranto.

Apart from these, families can also enjoy water parks, nature reserves, interactive farm visits, and more engaging experiences across Puglia.

CHAPTER 5

5-DAY ITINERARIES IN PUGLIA

Day 1: Trulli Exploration and Local Delights

Day 2: Coastal Charms and Cave Adventures

Day 3: Baroque Beauty and Wine Discoveries

Day 4: Seaside Serenity and Historical Monopoli

Day 5: Historical Gems and Urban Exploration

CHAPTER 5

5-DAY ITINERARIES IN PUGLIA

Day 1: Trulli Exploration and Local Delights

Morning: Dive into the unique Trulli of Alberobello, discovering their history on a guided tour. Enjoy local pastries and prosecco at Trulli e Puglia Wine Bar.

Afternoon: Immerse in Alberobello's culture with a Market Tour, a private cooking demo, and a visit to Trullo Sovrano.

Evening: Relish traditional Puglian dishes with a modern twist at Magnapulia. Finish with the Alberobello Dining Experience with locals.

Travel Tips: Wear comfortable shoes for exploring Alberobello's cobblestone streets. Book ahead for the Alberobello Dining Experience.

Day 2: Coastal Charms and Cave Adventures

Morning: Enjoy breakfast at Voglia... Pane e vino before exploring Polignano a Mare on a Private Culture and History Walking Tour.

Afternoon: Lunch with a view at Coccaro Beach Club, followed by a Stand-Up Paddle Board Sea Cave Trip.

Evening: Delight in a sophisticated dinner at Enoteca Divino and a romantic stroll along the dramatic Lama Monachile Bridge.

Travel Tips: Bring sunscreen and water for the paddleboarding trip. Check weather forecasts for ideal cave exploration.

Day 3: Baroque Beauty and Wine Discoveries

Morning: Discover the elegant streets of Martina Franca on a Private Tour. Enjoy breakfast at Le Stanzie.

Afternoon: Indulge in wine and local product tastings. Relax with lunch at Begula Club Café Restaurant.

Evening: Drive to Locorotondo for dinner at Cime di Tapas, followed by a charming stroll through the village.

Travel Tips: Wear comfortable footwear for exploring Locorotondo's cobblestone streets. Arrange transportation for the evening trip.

Day 4: Seaside Serenity and Historical Monopoli

Morning: Start with breakfast at Skipper bar. Explore Monopoli's history on a City Highlights Walking Tour with Tasting.

Afternoon: Relish lunch at Da Vittorino by Vecchi Marinai. Enjoy a Private Sightseeing Cruise with Champagne.

Evening: Dine at Tomarito by Pescaria and take a romantic walk along Cala Monaci.

Travel Tips: Bring a camera for capturing scenic views during the cruise. Reserve restaurant tables in advance.

Day 5: Historical Gems and Urban Exploration

Morning: Visit Bari Cruise Port and explore the city's historic heart on an Old Town Walking Tour. Visit the Swabian Castle and Bari Cathedral.

Afternoon: Lunch at Carlo Quinto, followed by a seaside stroll along the Promenade.

Evening: Conclude your trip with dinner at Classico - Bar all'Italiana | Ruvo di Puglia, savouring classic Italian dishes.

Travel Tips: Respect dress codes for historical sites. Allocate time for shopping in Bari's districts. Confirm restaurant reservations in advance.

CHAPTER 6

EXPLORING PUGLIA

Bari

Lecce

The Gargano

Peninsula

Gallipoli

Valle d'Itria

EXPLORING PUGLIA

Bari

Getting to Know Bari

Bari, the capital of the Metropolitan City of Bari and the Apulia region, is a captivating city located on the Adriatic Sea in southern Italy. Its history, filled with intriguing stories and tumultuous events, dates back to the Bronze Age, highlighting the city's ancient origins.

Originally a harbor of the Iapygian Peuceti, Bari experienced profound Greek influences before the Roman era, ultimately becoming an integral part of the Roman Republic. The city's Romanization further solidified its historical significance, evolving into a strategic point of junction between the coast road and the Via Traiana while serving as a pivotal port for eastward trade.

Bari earned the moniker "Gateway to the East" due to its enduring tradition of trade. Delving into the heart of the historic center unveils the city's authentic character, with echoes of its past intricately woven into the labyrinthine alleyways.

In the present day, Bari stands as a dynamic city, boasting its status as a vital university hub. It cherishes the memory of its seafaring exploits from the Middle Ages, reflected in its precious monuments and striking churches. The city comprises two distinct districts—the historic Bari Vecchia, or Old Bari, and the modern Città Nuova. The latter, laid out on a grid plan with wide, straight avenues, serves as the financial and administrative center, housing museums, theaters, concert halls, and the university. Via Sparano and Corso Cavour, alongside other vibrant streets, showcase Bari's modern charm, with fashionable labels and diverse shopping experiences contributing to the city's allure. Explore Bari's neighborhoods to unravel the layers of its rich historical tapestry.

Getting There & Getting Around

Air Travel

Bari Karol Wojtyła Airport: Located in southern Italy, it serves various cities across Italy and Europe. The airfare varies based on destinations and airlines, typically ranging from $215 to $333 for round-trip flights.

Train

Bari Centrale Station: This central train hub connects Bari to major Italian cities like Rome, Milan, Bologna, and Venice. While primarily used for connections to the airport and the Old Town area, it's a limited but efficient mode of transport. A monthly public transport pass costs approximately €37.31.

Taxi

Taxi Services: Easily accessible, companies like EuroTaxi, Puglia VIP, and Taxi Apulia offer services. The initial taxi fare is €3.22, while a one-hour trip costs around €21.29. The standard cost per kilometer is €0.886.

Shuttle

Shuttle Services: Providers like Apulia Shuttle and Shuttle Direct offer transfers to and from Bari International Airport Karol Wojtyła. The pricing varies based on the service type and distance traveled.

Bus

AMTAB Bus Line: Operates a route connecting the airport to Bari Central Station. A one-way ticket on public transport costs approximately €1.12. Most travelers use the bus once, primarily for airport-to-hotel or Old Town transport.

Places & Attraction Not to Miss

Bari Vecchia

Nestled between the old and new ports, Bari Vecchia is an enchanting labyrinth of medieval pathways, cobblestone alleys, and hidden courtyards teeming with an authentic charm. Wander through this atmospheric district on foot, exploring its rich tapestry of medieval architecture, small shrines, and quaint churches. The area feels like a world apart from the bustling modern city, offering a serene ambiance where local life unfolds in the streets. Delve into the sensory delights of the Old Town: discover hole-in-the-wall delis selling aromatic spices, cozy tavernas serving up bowls of cozze (mussels) and homemade pasta, and glimpses of housewives crafting traditional orecchiette pasta or frying sgagliozze (polenta squares) in the alleys. Embrace the local culinary scene, with Baresi enjoying sushi and indulging in freshly caught sea urchins and mussels at the vibrant fish market, washed down with chilled Peroni beer.

Marvel at the Medieval Castle during the enchanting sunset hours, where the area comes alive with the playful energy of children and pets. Piazza Mercantile and Piazza Ferrarese stand as the Old Town's bustling squares, with the former being the medieval trading center and the latter home to a friendly lion statue. Stroll along Via Venezia, an elevated walkway tracing the remains of the ancient city walls, and discover the Fortino di Sant'Antonio and Santa Scolastica, two bastions at either end. The Terracotta Teatro Margherita dominates the harbor, adding a unique architectural charm to Bari Vecchia.

While the district's intimate size means you won't stay lost for long, Corso Vittorio Emanuele II boasts a palm-lined pedestrian lane offering a glimpse into the area's vibrant life. Below this boulevard lies the Murat district, a modern grid of conveniences that's just a leisurely 10-minute walk from the train station, making navigation around the area effortlessly convenient.

San Nicola Basilica

Nestled in the heart of old Bari, the Basilica di San Nicola rises with an imposing presence, its austere fortress-like structure echoing tales of ancient relics and remarkable history. Dating back to the Italo-Norman era in Apulia, this basilica stands as one of the first grand Norman churches in Southern Italy, constructed between 1087 and 1197. Its genesis is intricately linked to the retrieval of Saint Nicholas' relics from Myra, present-day Turkey, safeguarding them from the threats of Saracen invasion. The basilica's magnificent edifice took over a century to complete, showcasing an architectural fusion of Byzantine influences and fortified elements characterized by its square appearance and stout towers that frame the facade. Inside, the grandeur unfolds with a nave and aisles, accentuated by granite columns and Byzantine-inspired arches that adorn the presbytery. For centuries, this revered site has drawn pilgrims from across the Christian world to the sanctity of the crypt where the remains of Saint Nicholas rest, making it a significant pilgrimage destination for both Roman Catholics and Orthodox Christians. The basilica's design served as a precedent, influencing numerous other constructions in the region standing as a testament to its enduring cultural and spiritual significance.

Norman-Swabian Castle

The Norman-Swabian Castle, dating back to 1132 under the reign of Norman King Roger II, holds an illustrious history etched in the ancient stones of Bari. Destroyed and rebuilt in 1156 by King William I of Sicily, its formidable walls were later reinforced in 1233 by the Holy Roman Emperor Frederick II. This architectural marvel, enclosed by a moat on three sides and once a seaside fortress, stands as a testament to medieval grandeur. Visitors crossing the bridge to its gate are transported to a realm where history meets contemporary cultural flair. Inside, amidst the Aragon walls and the central Hohenstaufen tower, the castle hosts captivating exhibitions, unveiling the rich tapestry of Bari's past. Wander through its corridors to discover archaeological remnants, ceramics, and the intriguing Gallery of Plaster Casts, which displays reproductions of medieval architectural elements. With its galleries and temporary displays, the castle invites travelers to delve into Bari's heritage and relish the charm of history intricately preserved within its walls. Open from Wednesday to Monday, between 8:30 AM and 7:30 PM, this castle offers an immersive experience that is a must-visit for history enthusiasts and architectural lovers alike.

Lungomare Nazario Sauro

Lungomare Nazario Sauro emerges as the quintessential promenade along the coastline of Bari, Italy, extending gracefully for approximately 1000 meters from the bustling harbor to the serene Parco per Cani. This enchanting walkway stands as the city's foremost seaside promenade, inviting visitors to indulge in its serene expanse. By day, bask in the Mediterranean sunshine while taking leisurely strolls or enjoying moments of relaxation amidst the coastal breeze. As dusk descends, the promenade transforms into a spectacle, offering a captivating panorama of the illuminated coastline. The path, adorned with remarkable architecture and whitewashed structures, exudes an irresistible charm that frames breathtaking views of the azure sea. Lungomare Nazario Sauro paints an idyllic picture of tranquility, beckoning travelers to revel in its beauty, whether under the vibrant daylight or the captivating night sky. Entrance to this scenic promenade is free and open to all, offering an inviting haven for those seeking a tranquil retreat along Bari's splendid waterfront.

Castello Normanno-Svevo

Standing as a testament to Bari's rich history, the Castello Normanno-Svevo, affectionately referred to as "u Castídde" in the local Barese dialect, holds a significant place as a historical fortress in Bari, Italy. Initially constructed by Norman King Roger II around 1132, the castle underwent a tumultuous history of destruction, rebuilding, and transformation under various rulers. It was revived and reinforced in 1233 by Frederick II during his reign as King of Sicily, boasting the imposing Aragon walls and the formidable Hohenstaufen tower. Resting on the edge of the western expanse, this Norman Swabian Castle, open Wednesday through Monday from 8:30 AM to 7:30 PM, now managed by the Ministry of Culture, serves as an exhibition space under the supervision of the Regional Directorate Museums of Puglia. Visitors crossing the bridge over the moat, transformed into a public garden, discover a treasure trove within. Inside, myriad exhibitions unveil archaeological remnants, ceramics, and the captivating Gallery of Plaster Casts, showcasing reproductions of medieval and post-medieval architectural marvels from renowned Puglian monuments and museums. Entrance fees vary, but this beautiful fortress offers a unique glimpse into Puglia's heritage, inviting exploration of its historical corridors and cultural exhibits.

The Cattedrale di San Sabino

The Cattedrale di San Sabino, also known as Bari Cathedral, stands as a profound testament to Bari's historical legacy, nestled in Italy's vibrant city of Bari. Originating from its initial construction around 1132 by Norman King Roger II, the cathedral encountered a series of destruction and renovation phases across centuries. Rebuilt and reinforced in 1233 by Frederick II, it evolved under varying rulers, witnessing transformations during the Angevin rule before being repurposed as a prison and barracks. The cathedral stands within the embrace of the Aragon walls and the prominent Hohenstaufen tower, encircled by a moat on every side except the northern edge, which overlooks the sea.

Today, the Ministry of Culture, under the Regional Directorate Museums of Puglia, diligently oversees the curation of this architectural wonder, providing engaging exhibitions. The cathedral, situated at Corso San Sabino, 1, Canosa Di Puglia, BT, 760122, greets visitors from Monday to Sunday, welcoming exploration from 09:00 to 12:30. Adorned with a majestic white facade and a soaring bell tower, the cathedral radiates timeless beauty against the backdrop of the azure sky. It pays homage to St. Sabinus, a revered bishop of Canosa, whose remains rest within the crypt. The interior echoes a transition from Baroque opulence to the authentic Puglian-Romanesque style, showcasing a captivating blend of history and architecture. Below the cathedral, the Museo del Succorpo della Cattedrale, a hidden gem, unfolds remnants of earlier structures, housing remarkable mosaics, tombs, and fragments of a Roman road, complemented by insightful English explanations. Opening hours may vary, offering visitors a fascinating journey through the heritage and relics of Bari's iconic cathedral.

5-Day Trip to Bari

DAY 1: Discovering Bari's Treasures

Morning: Explore Bari Vecchia, visiting the St. Nicholas Basilica and strolling through the charming streets. Take advantage of the Museo del Confetto Mucci Giovanni for traditional Italian sweets.

Afternoon: Enjoy a boat tour to Polignano a Mare, explore caves, and relish a seafood dinner at Al Pescatore.

Evening: Dive into Bari's nightlife with a Walking Street Food Tour and dinner at La Cecchina.

DAY 2: Castles and History

Morning: Visit the iconic Castel del Monte and the Swabian Castle in Bari for an insightful guided tour.

Afternoon: Drive to Trani, a coastal town with a stunning cathedral, and relish lunch at Osteria del Silbarno.

Evening: Enjoy a relaxing walk at Piazza del Ferrarese and authentic pizza at La Saghe.

DAY 3: Exploring Bari's Surroundings

Morning: Day trip to Gravina Di Puglia, exploring ancient cave dwellings and enjoying an Italian lunch at Botteghelle 65.

Afternoon: Learn pasta-making on the Bari Pasta Experience Walking Tour and take a bike tour with the Bari Bike-Rickshaw City Tour.

Evening: Have a romantic dinner at Osteria del Santissimo Rosario.

DAY 4: Coastal Beauty

Morning: Boat tour to Polignano a Mare, exploring caves, and having a seafood lunch at Pescatore di Mare.

Afternoon: Stroll around Polignano a Mare, enjoy a boat trip, and taste famous gelato at Mon Gâteau.

Evening: Return to Bari for a romantic dinner at La Brasserie.

DAY 5: Cultural Immersion

Morning: Begin with a Bari Segway Tour and gelato Tasting, then admire the city by boat with an Aperitivo.

Afternoon: Day trip to Matera to explore ancient cave dwellings and a traditional lunch at Hostaria Antico Trullo.

Evening: Conclude your journey with a goodbye dinner at Terrazza Masaniello, indulging in genuine Italian cuisine.

Travel Tips:

- Check for guided tours at attractions for better insights into history and culture.

- Book boat tours or activities in advance, especially during peak seasons.
- Enjoy local cuisines and gelato, they're a must-try!
- Use public transportation or taxis for longer distances between cities.
- Carry sunscreen and comfortable shoes for walking tours.
- Respect local customs and dining hours for a more immersive experience.

Where to Eat In Bari

Al Pescatore

Al Pescatore is a renowned seafood restaurant nestled in the heart of historic Bari, Italy. This charming eatery is celebrated for its exquisite and fresh seafood offerings, delivering a unique dining experience amidst vaulted ceilings and a captivating atmosphere. With a visible fish counter and a delightful veranda, it's an inviting spot for seafood enthusiasts. A meal here typically costs around €40 per person. You can reach the restaurant at +39 080 523 7039. Operating hours are from 13:00 to 15:00 and 20:00 to 23:00 on Monday, Wednesday, Thursday, Friday, and Sunday, while on Saturday, it's open from 13:00 to 15:00 and 20:00 to 00:00. Visit them at Piazza Federico II di Svevia 6, Bari, 70122, or check their website for more details. https://www.alpescatorebari.com/

Biancofiore

Biancofiore stands as a distinguished culinary gem nestled in the heart of Bari, Italy. Revered for its innovative take on traditional Pugliese cuisine, mainly focusing on seafood, this restaurant offers a captivating dining experience. Its charming ambiance, accentuated by stone walls reminiscent of Bari's old town's natural white tones and the azure sea, sets the stage for a memorable meal. A meal here typically costs around €38 per person. You can reach the restaurant at +39 080 523 5446. Operating hours are from 12:30 to 14:30 and 19:00 to 22:30 from Monday to Saturday. On Sundays, it's open from 12:30 - 15:00 and 19:00 to 22:30. You can find them at Corso Vittorio Emanuele II 13, Bari, 70122. For more details, visit https://www.ristorantebiancofiore.it/.

Per Bacco

Per Bacco stands as a hidden culinary treasure nestled in the heart of Bari, Italy. This charming fine dining establishment offers a delightful array of exquisite Puglian cuisine within a cozy and intimate setting. The interior boasts a blend of simplicity and elegance, adorned with vintage accents that echo a delightful wine-themed atmosphere. Typically, a meal here costs approximately €30-45 per person. To make reservations or inquiries, you can contact the restaurant at +39 080 558 8563. Operating hours are from 13:00 to 14:30 and 20:00 to 23:30, Monday to Friday, and from 20:00 to 23:30 on Saturdays. You'll find Per Bacco at Via Francesco Saverio Abbrescia 99, 70121, Bari, Italy.

Terranima

Terranima is a delightful restaurant situated in Bari, Italy, celebrated for its authentic Apulian cuisine. The welcoming ambiance, paired with a friendly staff, creates a homely atmosphere for visitors. The menu showcases a diverse array of regional specialties, including must-try dishes like orecchiette alle cime di rapa (pasta with turnip greens) and Melanzane Barisana (baked eggplant with ground beef sauce). A meal typically costs around €30-40 per person. For inquiries or reservations, you can contact the restaurant at +39 080 521 9725. They are operating hours span from 12:00 to 15:30 and 19:00 to 23:30, Monday through Saturday, and from 12:00 to 16:00 on Sundays. Terranima is located at Via Putignani, 213/215, Bari, 70122. For more comprehensive details, visit their website at https://www.terranima.com/

Il Sale

Il Sale stands as a top-rated seafood restaurant nestled in Bari, Italy, esteemed for its fresh, top-notch seafood dishes served in a modern, sophisticated setting. The approximate cost per person for a delightful meal here is around €28. To reach out or make reservations, contact the restaurant at +39 080 522 8959. Operating hours span from 09:00 to 23:00, Monday through Saturday. You'll find Il Sale situated at 50-52 Marchese di Montrone Street, Bari, 70122. For a more detailed insight into their offerings, visit their website at https://www.ilsaleristorante.it/

Lecce

Getting To Know Lecce

Lecce, often dubbed the "Florence of the South," sits nestled in the heart of Salento within Apulia's enchanting Southern Italy. Renowned for its profound historical tapestry, architectural marvels, and vibrant cultural legacy, Lecce holds an intriguing allure.

Tracing its roots back to antiquity, Lecce's origins are shrouded in time, dating as far as the 5th century BC or perhaps even further, according to legend, linking its genesis to the aftermath of Troy's fall. The city thrived during Roman dominion, witnessing grand architectural undertakings like the Roman Theatre and Amphitheatre.

Following the decline of the post-Roman Empire, Lecce's fortunes rose anew with the Normans' arrival, heralding an era of resurgence. Emerging as a pivotal county and eventually Salento's capital, Lecce flourished under the Kingdom of Naples' governance, evolving into a vibrant cultural nexus and a global trading hub.

Lecce's architectural charm lies in its distinctive Baroque style, the famed "Lecce Baroque," an artistic expression deeply rooted in Mediterranean aesthetics. The city's allure is further enhanced by its exquisite columns, arches, intricate rose windows, quaint squares, and labyrinthine alleyways.

Today, Lecce remains a bustling city, teeming with a tapestry of creative events and cherished traditional celebrations. Its streets weave together artistic marvels from the Roman, Medieval, and Renaissance periods, painting a vibrant portrait of history and culture. Lecce, with its rich

93

tapestry of historical heritage and artistic flair, invites visitors to immerse themselves in its timeless allure and vibrant contemporary spirit.

Getting There & Getting Around

Air Travel: For those arriving by air, Brindisi Airport (BDS) serves as the nearest airport to Lecce. Airlines like easyJet, ITA Airways, and Swiss International Air Lines operate flights to BDS. Ticket prices for a one-way journey to Lecce start around $43, while round-trip fares can begin at $86.

Train Travel: Lecce boasts excellent train connectivity serviced by Trenitalia and Italo. Travellers can embark on local train rides within Puglia or even journeys from far-off locations like London, which can take approximately 26 hours and 49 minutes. The cost of train travel varies based on distance and train type.

Taxi Services: Several taxi companies, such as Taxi 12 Lecce, RadioTaxi Lecce, and Cooperativa Taxi Lecce, offer services in the city. A typical starting tariff for a taxi ride is around €5, with additional charges of approximately €2.25 per mile and a waiting charge of about €20 per hour.

Shuttle Services: Transport to and from the airport or other destinations is facilitated by shuttle services like Taurino Shuttle, Salento Viaggi & Air Shuttle, and Puglia Shuttle. Costs may fluctuate based on distance and the specific service required.

Bus Services: SGM manages the local bus services in Lecce. A one-way bus ticket costs around €1, making it an economical choice for city exploration. Monthly passes are also available, ranging between €29 and €35, allowing unlimited travel around Lecce and its neighbouring areas.

Places & Attractions to Explore In Lecce

The Centro Storico

The Centro Storico, or Historical Center, stands as an essential gem in Puglia, steeped in history and adorned with captivating Baroque architecture. As you wander through its labyrinthine streets, you'll find yourself amidst an open-air museum, where the past breathes life into the present. The narrow passageways adorned with ancient facades lead to breathtaking squares and concealed courtyards, revealing the city's vibrant tapestry of culture and local traditions. The heart of this historic hub lies in Piazza della Libertà, a lively square pulsating with the rhythm of local life. Delve into the Chiesa dello Spirito Santo, a stunning church showcasing intricate designs and rich history. The Palazzo dell'Universita e Torre dell'orologio, an eminent university building crowned by a majestic clock tower, echoes tales of eras past. Not to miss is the iconic Colonna Di Sant'oronzo, a monument standing proud and symbolizing the city's enduring legacy.

Teatro Romano

Nestled within the heart of Puglia's historic centre lies the Teatro Romano, a breathtakingly well-preserved Roman amphitheatre that serves as an exquisite testament to the region's illustrious past. Located in the charming Piazza Sant'Oronzo, this hidden gem not only showcases impressive architectural prowess but also unravels the splendour of classical Roman life through the myriad artefacts unearthed during its excavation. Adjacent to this marvel stands the Museo Teatro Romano, a haven for history enthusiasts, housing a trove of these unearthed treasures while masterfully recreating scenes depicting the opulence of Roman Lupiae (Lecce).

Visitors can revel in the allure of Piazza Sant'Oronzo, a vibrant square offering a splendid view of the amphitheatre, before delving into the mesmerizing tapestry of the Historical Center through immersive walking tours. Amidst exploration, savouring local street food becomes an integral part of the experience, allowing a taste of authentic Puglian flavours while traversing the city's streets.

Furthermore, this captivating site serves as a springboard to nearby attractions that promise to enrich the journey through Puglia. From the architectural marvel of the Basilica di Santa Croce to the historical allure of the Museo Faggiano and the grandeur of the Cathedral, these nearby gems enhance the overall tapestry of exploration within close proximity to the Teatro Romano. Indulge in a journey through time and revel in the captivating blend of history, art, and culture nestled within the vibrant embrace of Puglia's Teatro Romano and its surrounding wonders.

Piazza Sant'Oronzo

Nestled at the heart of Lecce, Piazza Sant'Oronzo stands as the vibrant nucleus of the city's historic centre, captivating visitors with its lively ambience and rich tapestry of activities. This bustling square serves as more than a mere gathering spot; it's a cultural hotspot brimming with cafes, restaurants, gelaterias, and shops that not only invite indulgence but also offer an ideal vantage point for leisurely people-watching sessions. Throughout the year, the square transforms into a dynamic stage hosting a myriad of events, showcasing the city's vibrant spirit and cultural heritage. Beyond its bustling energy, the piazza boasts remarkable attractions, including the restored 2nd-century-AD Roman Amphitheater, nestled below ground level, offering a glimpse into ancient history. The iconic Column of Sant'Oronzo, marking the historic end of the Appian Way in Brindisi, adds a touch of antiquity to the square's allure. For those seeking a panoramic view and modern comforts, L'attico Piazza Sant'Oronzo, a bed and breakfast, provides an inviting retreat.

Additionally, the Infopoint Lecce Sedile stands as a beacon for tourists, offering event schedules and local insights. While immersing yourself in the vibrant atmosphere of the square, relish the opportunity to sample mouth-watering local delicacies at the plethora of cafes and restaurants that adorn this captivating hub. Piazza Sant'Oronzo, with its dynamic ambience and cultural treasures, remains a quintessential highlight, offering an immersive and delightful experience within the heart of Lecce.

The Basilica di Santa Croce

The Basilica di Santa Croce in Lecce is a shining example of the city's magnificent Baroque style. This stunning church, built painstakingly between 1549 and 1699, exudes beauty both on its intricate exterior and within its breathtaking interior. Adorned with intricate carvings depicting a menagerie of motifs—from sheep and dodos to cherubs and fantastical creatures—the facade mesmerizes with its 16th and 17th-century artistry, offering a swirling, magnificent allegorical feast. Step inside to discover a more conventionally Baroque interior adorned with exquisite paintings and a collection of 16 altars, among which the one in the left transept stands as a pinnacle masterpiece of Baroque artistry in the south.

Beyond its architectural magnificence, the basilica invites exploration of its interior artwork, showcasing breathtaking depictions of the Adoration of the Shepherds, the Annunciation, the Visit of Mary to St. Elizabeth, and the Flight to Egypt. Wander through the halls to explore the intricate altars and side chapels, each a testament to artistic brilliance and religious devotion. Nearby, within a short distance, lies a tapestry of attractions, including the Lecce Roman Amphitheatre, the Church of Saint Irene, and the Lecce Cathedral, enriching the journey through the city's historical treasures.

While indulging in the cultural and architectural splendour, take time to savour local delicacies at the numerous cafes and restaurants surrounding this breathtaking landmark. The Basilica di Santa Croce, with its ornate facade, captivating interior, and neighbouring attractions, stands tall as a quintessential destination, inviting visitors to immerse themselves in the rich tapestry of Puglia's artistic and historical heritage.

The Cattedrale dell'Assunzione della Virgine

The Cattedrale dell'Assunzione della Virgine, famously known as the Lecce Cathedral, stands as a remarkable testament to Puglia's rich history and architectural brilliance. Initially constructed in 1144, with subsequent renovations and a complete Baroque reconstruction in the 17th century, this cathedral devoted to the Assumption of the Virgin Mary serves not only as a symbol of religious reverence but also as the spiritual heart of Lecce. Its Baroque architecture captivates visitors, showcasing two distinct entrances—the elegant north side and the intricately carved Baroque portal facing the square, a stunning display of craftsmanship. Step inside to marvel at the cathedral's interior adorned with painted wooden ceilings in the nave and transepts, and explore its 12 chapels, notably the striking Cappella Sant'Oronzo. Don't overlook the impressive 70-meter-high bell tower, a prominent feature added during the cathedral's Baroque-era reconstruction. Surrounding the cathedral, the Piazza del Duomo beckons exploration alongside other significant religious buildings, including the Basilica di Santa Croce, enriching the cultural and historical tapestry of the city. Amidst the exploration, relish the opportunity to sample delectable local delicacies at the array of cafes and restaurants that adorn the nearby square, adding a flavorful touch to the cathedral's enriching visit.

The Castello di Lecce

The Castello di Lecce, also known as Castello Carlo V, stands as a historic gem within Puglia, tracing its origins to the 12th century under Norman rule and later expanded by Charles V in the 16th century. This impressive castle, nestled at XXV Luglio Street in Lecce, boasts colossal trapezoidal walls and formidable bastions, encapsulating the region's rich history within its walls. As the largest castle in Puglia, it has morphed from a prison and military barracks to its current role as the headquarters of Lecce's cultural authorities. Visitors can immerse themselves in its historical aura, exploring its architectural grandeur and delving into the local artistry showcased at the on-site papier-mâché museum. Cultural aficionados can partake in recitals and events hosted within its storied confines. For those eager to visit, the castle operates from Monday to Friday, welcoming guests from 09:00 to 20:30, and on weekends from 09:30 to 20:30. To reach out or inquire about admission fees and details, contact the castle at 0832 2465174 or via email at info@castellodilecce.it. While in the area, seize the opportunity to explore neighboring attractions like the Basilica di Santa Croce, Museo Faggiano, the Roman Amphitheater, and relish the flavors of local cuisine at the surrounding cafes and restaurants. The Castello di Lecce stands as a testament to the region's rich heritage, inviting travelers to immerse themselves in its historical tapestry and cultural significance. Website: www.castellocarlov.it

Villa Comunale di Lecce

The vibrant hub of Salento in Puglia lies the Villa Comunale di Lecce, also known as the Giardini Pubblici di Giuseppe Garibaldi, a serene haven offering respite from the city's lively atmosphere. Established in 1818, this captivating city park sprawls across three hectares, enchanting visitors with its ornate fountains, a charming bandstand, and meticulously manicured gardens. It's a sanctuary ideal for strolls, inviting visitors to unwind and immerse themselves in a tranquil ambience amidst nature's embrace.

Within the park's enchanting confines, discover a large two-section fountain, a picturesque bridge, neoclassical buildings, and a monument honouring Garibaldi, adding historical depth to this scenic oasis. Positioned close to prominent attractions like Piazza del Duomo, Lecce Cathedral, and Basilica Santa Croce, the Villa Comunale di Lecce serves as a gateway to a tapestry of cultural and historical marvels within easy reach.

The park extends a warm welcome to visitors every day from 08:00 to 21:00, providing plenty of time to discover and enjoy its serene beauty and peaceful surroundings. Located at Viale 25 Luglio, 73100 in Lecce, visitors can contact the park administration at 0832 6821113 for inquiries.

Mura Urbiche di Lecce

Situated at Via Leonardo Leo 1, 73100 in Lecce, the Mura Urbiche di Lecce stands as a pivotal attraction in Puglia, echoing the city's storied past and architectural finesse of the 16th century. These ancient city walls, masterminded by military architect Gian Giacomo Dell'Acaya, were erected as formidable defences for Lecce, preserving a slice of history waiting to be explored. Guided tours offer a captivating journey through time, inviting visitors to immerse themselves in the rich tapestry of the city's heritage.

Within the vicinity, the main square boasts a stunning Baroque Church, majestic Palaces, and the Town Hall, inviting exploration into their historical grandeur. The Palazzo del Principe entices with castle dungeons adorned with medieval prisoners' wall drawings. At the same time, the Museo Diffuso di Borgo Terra delves deeper into the dungeons, unveiling tales etched by incarcerated souls.

Opening its doors from Monday to Saturday, welcoming guests from 08:30 to 23:00, and on Sundays from 14:00 to 23:00, the Mura Urbiche di Lecce offers admission at €5.00, with a reduced rate of €3.00 for children aged 12 to 17. For further details, inquiries, and guided tour schedules, reach out to them at 0832 6829851 or visit their official website at https://www.muraurbiche.it/.

Museo Diocesano

The Museo Diocesano stands as an essential stop in Puglia, inviting visitors to immerse themselves in a treasury of religious art and historical artifacts. Nestled in Piazza del Duomo, 73100, Lecce, Italy, this museum encapsulates the rich cultural tapestry of the region, offering a captivating journey through its exhibits. Among the top attractions within this cultural trove, the archaeological exhibition "Lo spreco necessario" stands out, showcasing archaeological discoveries spanning five decades. Delve into "The Polychromies of the Sublime," a mesmerizing collection of marble sculptures dating back to the second half of the 4th century B.C., echoing the artistic prowess of ancient times. Operating from 10:00 AM to 1:00 PM, the museum provides a window into Puglia's heritage.

5-Day Trip In Lecce

Day 1: Exploring Lecce's Historical Sites

Morning: Begin with a guided tour of the iconic Lecce Basilica of Santa Croce and the well-preserved Lecce Roman Amphitheatre.

Afternoon: Relish traditional cuisine at Petrini for lunch, then explore Porta Napoli and landmarks like Lecce Cathedral and Church of Saint Irene.

Evening: Dive into a street food tour, sampling local delights. End your day with a delightful dinner at Osteria degli Spiriti.

Travel Tip: Wear comfortable shoes for walking tours.

Day 2: Discovering Lecce's Culture and Art

Morning: Hop on a bike for a tour encompassing the Faggiano Museum and Lecce's Baroque Architecture.

Afternoon: Learn Apulian culinary secrets in a cooking lesson. Follow up with a rickshaw tour of hidden gems.

Evening: Savor authentic dishes at Trattoria Nonna Tetti. Then, indulge in a wine-tasting experience at Tormaresca Vigneti e Fattorie.

Travel Tip: Carry sunscreen and water during outdoor tours.

Day 3: Day Trip to Alberobello, Locorotondo, and Ostuni

Morning: Venture on a full-day trip exploring Alberobello's trulli houses, Locorotondo's charming streets, and Ostuni's striking architecture.

Afternoon: Relish a local lunch at Il Cortiletto in Ostuni and leisurely explore its historic center.

Evening: Return to Lecce for a family-run dinner at Le Zie. Embrace Lecce's lively nightlife scene.

Travel Tip: Wear comfortable clothes and shoes for walking tours.

Day 4: Lecce's Culinary Delights and Jewish History

Morning: Dive into Lecce's street food scene and explore Jewish heritage on a walking tour.

Afternoon: Enjoy lunch at Mamma Elvira and browse local markets for unique souvenirs.

Evening: Savor fresh seafood at Osteria da Angiulino and unwind at Alle Scale with live music.

Travel Tip: Keep local currency handy for market shopping.

Day 5: Farewell to Lecce

Morning: Cycle through the scenic countryside on a wine tour and uncover hidden city gems via a rickshaw-guided tour.

Afternoon: Delight in a casual lunch at Pai & Fusti, then walk along the city walls for panoramic views.

Evening: Conclude your journey with a fusion dinner at Osteria degli Artisti and unwind at the Uarije lounge bar.

Travel Tip: Plan transportation to the airport or your next destination in advance.

The Gargano Peninsula

Getting to Know The Gargano Peninsula

The Gargano Peninsula, often referred to as the "spur" of Italy's boot, stands as a hidden gem within Puglia, offering a historical and geographical journey in the province of Foggia. This isolated mountain massif, boasting highlands and peaks, forms the backbone of the Gargano Promontory, extending into the Adriatic Sea. Dominated by the imposing Monte Calvo at 1,065 meters, the peninsula is bathed by the Adriatic on three sides, encompassing the enchanting Gargano National Park, established in 1991.

The Gargano Peninsula allures visitors with its rugged limestone cliffs, sandy beaches, captivating caves, and mesmerizing blue-green waters, forming a breathtaking coastline. On the contrary, its densely forested inland area, especially the Foresta Umbra, safeguards the remnants of an ancient oak and beech forest reminiscent of the woodlands that once blanketed a significant part of Central Europe.

Beyond its natural beauty, the Gargano Peninsula is a treasure trove of history and culture. The oldest shrine in Western Europe dedicated to the archangel Michael, Monte Sant'Angelo sul Gargano, stands as a testament to the region's spiritual heritage. The peninsula's archaeological sites, historic buildings, and museums offer a glimpse into its rich past.

Immerse yourself in the vibrant local culture by participating in the numerous festivals and events that punctuate the Gargano Peninsula's calendar. Engage in the daily life of coastal towns, where the warmth of the locals and the allure of their traditions add another layer to the region's charm.

Whether hiking in the Gargano National Park, exploring historic sites, or relaxing on beautiful beaches, the peninsula offers diverse activities for visitors. Monte Sant'Angelo beckons history enthusiasts, while water sports enthusiasts can indulge in the stunning coastal offerings. The

Gargano Peninsula is a haven for culinary enthusiasts. Explore the local cuisine in charming restaurants and cafes, savoring delicious dishes made from the region's renowned olive oil and wines. Take advantage of the chance to embark on tastings and tours offered by local producers.

The Gargano Peninsula, though slightly off the beaten path, rewards those who venture. Be prepared for slow travel, especially from the gateway city of Manfredónia. Plan your visit during quieter months like October for a more tranquil experience. As you explore, embrace the rich history, natural wonders, and warm hospitality that define this captivating region in Puglia.

Getting to and Around Gargano Peninsula

By Air: The closest airport to Gargano Peninsula is Bari Airport, approximately 115 miles from Vieste, a key city in the region. Upon arrival, renting a car at the airport is a popular choice for travellers looking to explore the peninsula.

Train Services: Trains from Bari connect to Manfredonia and San Severo, acting as gateways to Gargano. However, it's essential to note that Gargano itself doesn't have railway lines. From Manfredonia to San Severo, buses provide connections to various parts of the peninsula.

Taxi Services: In Gargano, reliable taxi services such as Taxi San Giovanni Rotondo and Taxi Express Aurora operate. Taxi rates can fluctuate depending on the distance travelled and the time of day, providing convenient transportation options within the area.

Shuttle Services: Available shuttle services facilitate easy transportation between different towns and attractions, providing a hassle-free travel option for visitors exploring the peninsula.

Bus Services: Companies like SITA and ATAF offer bus services connecting towns across the Gargano Peninsula. These buses serve as an alternative to train travel, providing convenient inter-town transportation.

Costs: Renting a car from Bari Airport could start at around €30-40 per day. Taxi fares within Gargano may range from €10-30 for shorter distances. Shuttle services and bus tickets might vary from €5-15 depending on the route.

Exploring The Place & Attractions

Monte Sant'Angelo

Nestled atop one of Gargano's highest mountains, Monte Sant'Angelo at Via Reale Basilica, 127, 71037 Monte Sant'Angelo (FG) Italy, stands as a prominent attraction within the Gargano Peninsula. This town boasts unparalleled panoramic vistas that stretch across the Gargano region. Drenched in history, it showcases a wealth of architecturally significant monuments.

Monte Sant'Angelo is adorned with historical marvels, including the renowned Sanctuary of San Michele Arcangelo, the impressive Castle, and the Tomba di Rotari. The Sanctuary, erected on the site of the Archangel Michael's apparition in a cave, stands as a spiritual testament. The Castle, with bastions from different eras, commands a dominating presence, overlooking the town from its pinnacle. The Tomba di Rotari, an imposing domed tower, is steeped in tradition as the alleged tomb of Rothari, a Lombard chieftain.

The town's museums welcome visitors from 9:00 AM - 12:15 PM and from 3:00 PM to 7:00 PM. Admission to the Castle is a mere 2 euros, granting access to its historical treasures. For more information or inquiries, contact Monte Sant'Angelo at +39 0884 561150. Monte Sant'Angelo, recognized as a World Heritage site, enchants travellers with its picturesque old quarter adorned with meandering alleys and stunning monuments. Perched at 800 meters (2,625 feet), this pilgrimage town offers breathtaking vistas over the Bay of Manfredónia.

Santuario di San Michele Arcangelo

Nestled in the heart of the Gargano Peninsula at Via Reale Basilica 127, 71037 Monte Sant'Angelo, Italy, the Santuario di San Michele Arcangelo stands as a revered historic site and one of the most sacred cave churches globally. Set atop a hill amidst the lush greenery of Gargano's landscapes, this Sanctuary holds profound spiritual significance. The façade, adorned with two arches and a niche housing the statue of San Michele, exudes an air of grace and reverence. Accessible from the vestibule, a staircase leads

109

visitors to the sacred cave, a place of deep devotion and historical significance.

The Sanctuary's highlights encompass the awe-inspiring grotto cave structure and its elegant access. Dating back to 1490, the site holds profound religious importance, attributed to the apparitions of the Archangel Michael. The Sanctuary ensures accessibility, offering a lift for those with mobility constraints. Open year-round, entry to the Sanctuary is free. However, guided tours inside the crypt can be booked, and a nominal fee grants access to the holy museum and lapidary museum within the Sanctuary.

The Santuario di San Michele Arcangelo welcomes visitors from 7:30 am to 7:30 pm, with potentially shorter hours in the off-season.

For further details or to arrange visits and guided tours, contact them at +390884561150 or visit their website:https://www.santuariosanmichele.it/. The Sanctuary encapsulates a profound spiritual experience, offering a journey into history and devotion within the captivating cave where the Archangel Michael is believed to have appeared to the Bishop of Siponto. The ornate double-arched Gothic portico and the magnificent bronze doors depicting biblical scenes lead visitors down 86 steps into the dimly lit Sanctuary. Within the grotto lie a 16th-century statue of the Archangel and a 12th-century marble episcopal throne steeped in historical and religious significance.

Foresta Umbra

Nestled within the Gargano National Park in Monte Sant'Angelo, 71037, the Foresta Umbra stands as a captivating gem in the heart of the Gargano Peninsula. Spanning 15,000 acres, this ancient forest of oak, beech, chestnut, and Aleppo pines is a haven of biodiversity, preserving the last remaining forest of its kind in Italy. The Foresta Umbra is a sanctuary for extinct animal breeds, offering a pristine habitat for wildlife. Visitors are invited to immerse themselves in the natural splendour through activities such as hiking, mountain biking, and wildlife viewing.

The forest unfolds its wonders through various attractions, including the mesmerizing artificial lake, the enchanting deer reserve, and a small naturalistic museum. With 15 marked trails catering to different levels of expertise, from beginners to avid trekkers and mountain bikers, Foresta Umbra offers a diverse range of exploration options. The forest welcomes visitors year-round with open arms, and admission is free. However, the naturalistic museum opens exclusively during the summer months, providing additional insights into the region's flora and fauna.

For further inquiries or to plan your visit, contact Foresta Umbra at +39 0884 560944 or visit their website at https://www.puglia.com/cosa-vedere/. This ancient wooded expanse, the only actual forested area in Puglia, boasts a rich tapestry of beech, chestnut, Aleppo pines, and oak trees. A habitat for deer, foxes, hares, and a myriad of indigenous orchids, Foresta Umbra offers marked trails that have become increasingly popular for guided hiking and cycling tours. As a vital component of the Gargano

National Park, the Foresta Umbra beckons nature enthusiasts and adventurers alike to discover the unparalleled beauty of this protected region.

Gargano National Park

Nestled in the province of Foggia, southern Italy, the Gargano National Park, established in 1991, stands as Apulia's largest sanctuary of natural wonders and historical treasures. Spanning across the Gargano promontory, the historic woodlands of Foresta Umbra, the Tremiti Islands archipelago, and the picturesque Lago Salso wetlands, this park offers a diverse range of outdoor activities. Visitors can engage in hiking, mountain biking, wildlife observation, and captivating boat excursions.

Within this expansive park lie captivating destinations like the coastal towns of Vieste and Peschici, the enchanting Foresta Umbra, the elevated village of Monte Sant'Angelo, and the serene Tremiti Islands. Adorned with the last surviving oak and beech tree forest in Italy, the park mesmerizes with its biodiversity and stunning landscapes.

The Gargano National Park, situated at SP50, 71010 - Carpino, welcomes visitors throughout the year. While the park remains accessible at all times, the museum operates from April to October. Entrance to the park is usually free, although certain attractions might have nominal fees. For more details, visit the Park's website at https://www.parcogargano.it/. Explore this pristine haven, teeming with natural wonders and historical gems, offering an immersive experience in Apulia's diverse and captivating landscapes.

Vieste

Vieste, the largest resort in the Gargano Peninsula, beckons travellers to explore its captivating charm in the heart of Puglia. Positioned on the tip of the peninsula, Vieste boasts a breathtaking backdrop of caves, cliffs, and golden beaches. The town offers an array of activities, from enchanting boat trips along the cave-riddled coast to captivating excursions to the Isole Tremiti. Despite tourist development on the outskirts, Vieste preserves its allure with a historic quarter featuring whitewashed houses, medieval alleys, and arches. The skyline is graced by the Romanesque cathedral, witness to centuries of remodelling, and the castle, a creation of Frederick II, perched at the town's highest point. Regrettably, the castle is not open to the public.

Beaches

The Gargano Peninsula in Puglia stands as a paradise for beach enthusiasts, boasting some of Italy's most stunning coastal stretches. These beaches offer a delightful mix of serene relaxation and thrilling water activities. Whether you seek sun-drenched lounging, leisurely swims, or exciting water sports, the beaches along the Gargano Peninsula cater to all preferences. Among the top beaches to explore are Baia delle Zagare, Spiaggia di Vignanotica, and Cala Tonda. In Vieste, renowned for its coastal charm, two standout beaches include the expansive Spiaggia di Pizzomunno to the south, named after its towering 20-meter rock monolith, and the vast Spiaggia di Scialmarino, situated 4.5 kilometres (north. Some beaches are within walking distance, adorned post-August with fewer visitors and rows of sun loungers and parasols that begin to dwindle.

Peschici

Nestled as a captivating cliff-clinging town resembling the charm of Amalfi, Peschici stands out as a premier destination within the Gargano Peninsula. The town's allure is defined by its stunning marina and the captivating Zaiana Beach. While the historic Castello di Peschici is a significant landmark, regrettably, it remains closed to the public. However, the castle, perched at Recinto Baronale 1, 71010 - Peschici, offers sweeping views and operates from Monday to Sunday, with visiting hours from 09:30 to 13:30 and 16:30 to 00:00. Contact them at 0884 964078 for further details. Another notable sacred site is the Abbey of Santa Maria di Kalena. For an exceptional experience, consider engaging with TRAVEL-TO-TREMITI: T.T.T., website:https://www.peschicitourismservice.com/, a local tourist service agency reachable at 0884 962573. Travelling to Peschici from Vieste via the S.S. 89 unfolds picturesque vistas of olive groves and winding mountain roads before descending upon this charming fishing town. Peschici, more intimate than Vieste, reveals a lively historic centre, a hilltop castle, and numerous avenues vending esteemed Pugliese products, including renowned local olive oil. Delve into the world of olive oil at Al Vecchio Frantoio, which houses an old olive press and offers tastings, including specialty lemon-flavoured oil. Ascending from there, the

114

cobbled streets lead to Castello di Peschici, which is open from June to September. It houses a museum with a historical collection of torture devices, adding an intriguing layer to its 10th-century origins.

The Isole Tremiti

Resting within the shimmering Adriatic Sea, the Isole Tremiti presents itself as a stunning archipelago nestled within the Gargano Peninsula. Celebrated for their natural beauty and pristine, transparent waters, these islands provide a multitude of activities and attractions for visitors to enjoy. Among the top draws is the breathtaking Faro di San Domino, a picturesque lighthouse situated on the island of San Domino. Don't miss Cala delle Arene, the islands' singular sandy beach known for its tropical ambience and stunningly azure waters. Water sports enthusiasts can revel in offerings by Marlin Tremiti and Mare e Stelle, both providing scuba diving and captivating boat tours. Mare e Stelle, positioned at Strada del Porto, Tremiti Islands, 710515, operates from Monday to Sunday, welcoming visitors from 09:00 to 19:00. For further inquiries, contact them at 371 489 1806. The archipelago, situated 22 kilometres north of the Gargano Peninsula, boasts a landscape characterized by jagged white cliffs, sandy coves, and sparkling grottoes lining the coastline. Notably, only two of the five islands are inhabited, hosting a modest population of around 200 residents.

Gallipoli

Getting to know Gallipoli

Gallipoli, a captivating town in Puglia, unfolds a compelling tale of history and culture that echoes through the ages. Recognized as a city of Greater Greece, Gallipoli held sway over an expansive territory, including the present-day Porto Cesareo, a testament to its historical significance. In the annals of 265 BC, Gallipoli aligned itself with Pyrrhus and Taranto in opposition to ancient Rome, resulting in a defeat that relegated it to a Roman colony. Positioned on a peninsula where the Dardanelles meet the Sea of Marmara, Gallipoli evolved into a crucial Byzantine fortress and later became the inaugural Ottoman conquest in Europe, serving as a strategic naval base.

The remnants of ancient ruins coexist harmoniously with the vibrant energy of its piazzas, offering travellers a distinctive experience. Whether wandering through the historic city centre or savouring the local gastronomy, visitors find themselves immersed in the cultural richness that defines this enchanting Italian town. The echoes of Gallipoli's past resonate in every cobblestone street, inviting exploration and appreciation for a history that has shaped the city into the unique destination it is today.

Getting to & Around Gallipoli

Getting to and around Gallipoli offers a variety of transportation options for travellers. The closest airport is in Brindisi, accessible through several airlines like easyJet, ITA Airways, and Swiss International Air Lines, offering roundtrip prices ranging from $72 to $152, with one-way tickets starting at $34. From Brindisi, travellers can take private transfers or shuttle services like Salento Shuttle to reach Gallipoli.

The town is served by the Ferrovia del Sud Est rail and bus lines. To arrive by train, take a regular train to Lecce from Foggia or Brindisi and then transfer to the Ferrovia del Sud Est line to Gallipoli. Italo Train also offers routes from Bologna and Florence to Gallipoli starting at €29.9 and €31.9, respectively.

For local transportation, Gallipoli offers numerous taxi services, such as Navetta Taxi, Gallipoli Servizio Aeroporto H245, Gallipoli Transfer, and Navetta Lu Salento Gallipoli. Prices for taxis vary based on distance and travel time. Shuttle services, like Salento Shuttle and Gallipoli Transfer, provide private transfers from airports or Lecce to Gallipoli, as well as guided tours to explore Salento.

Within Gallipoli, several bus companies, including FlixBus, Marino Autolinee, Sais Autolinee, Itabus, and Miccolis, operate. The central bus station is located at Via Firenze in Gallipoli, offering varying prices depending on travel distance and time. These transportation options afford travellers flexibility in exploring Gallipoli's attractions and neighbouring areas while enjoying the convenience of different modes of travel.

Exploring Gallipoli

Sea Tour Gallipoli

Sea Tour Gallipoli stands as a premier attraction, enticing visitors to delve into the mesmerizing natural landscapes of the Salento Natural Parks. Nestled at Via Santa Cristina, 1, Gallipoli, Infopoint turistico, Gallipoli, 73014, this tour offers a gateway to the region's stunning coastal beauty. Delve into the crystalline waters, exploring hidden coves and serene bays while indulging in a myriad of activities such as captivating boat tours, thrilling excursions, snorkelling escapades, lively boat parties, and tranquil sunset aperitifs. Whether you're after adventurous voyages or peaceful moments by the sea, Sea Tour Gallipoli curates an unforgettable experience, inviting travellers to immerse themselves in the breathtaking natural beauty of Salento's charms. For more information or bookings, contact them at 351 811 9050.

The Castle of Gallipoli

The Castle of Gallipoli stands as a premier attraction in the town, providing visitors with an exceptional window into its rich historical tapestry. This fortress, positioned entirely surrounded by the sea, offers not only stunning panoramic views but also an immersive journey through time. Located at Imbriani Square, Gallipoli, Lecce, 73014, the castle serves as a testament to the town's strategic significance. Unfortunately, specific hours of operation and admission fees might vary, so it's advisable to contact them directly at 0833 262775 for the most accurate and up-to-date information.

The Centro Storico di Gallipoli

The Centro Storico di Gallipoli stands as a pinnacle attraction in the town, providing visitors with an extraordinary opportunity to delve into its rich historical fabric. This historic city centre is a trove of cultural heritage, brimming with iconic landmarks and sites that offer a captivating glimpse into Gallipoli's past. Located at 23 Via Incrociata, Gallipoli, LE, 73014, the Centro Storico is a labyrinth of narrow streets adorned with ancient architecture and historical treasures. Exploring this area unveils a wealth of experiences, from wandering along quaint alleys to visiting historical monuments. Unfortunately, specific hours of operation and admission fees might vary, so for the most accurate and current information, it's recommended to contact them directly at 345 215 3876.

Valle d'Itria

Getting to Know Valle d'Itria

Valle d'Itria, nestled in the heart of Puglia in Southern Italy, stands as a captivating region steeped in unique cultural and historical significance.

Spanning across the provinces of Bari, Brindisi, and Taranto, this area encompasses a stunning landscape adorned with traditional towns like Martina Franca, Locorotondo, Cisternino, and Ceglie Messapica. Despite its name as a "valley," it's actually a depression formed by karstic phenomena, offering a breathtaking backdrop that's both traditional and stunning.

Historically, the name "Itria" is linked to the Basilian Fathers' oriental cult of the Madonna Odegitria, the guiding patron of travellers. They founded a monastic site in the valley, and an iconic fresco depicting the Madonna Odegitria was uncovered, adding to the region's rich historical tapestry.

What truly defines Valle d'Itria is the mesmerizing presence of "Trulli," ancient Apulian tiny round stone houses topped with conical roofs. These architectural marvels, set amidst the olive groves and vineyards, contribute to the area's distinct charm, creating an enchanting setting that is quintessentially Valle d'Itria. The town of Alberobello, a UNESCO World Heritage site, proudly showcases these trulli in abundance. In contrast, other villages offer a more serene, natural setting where these unique structures blend seamlessly with the surrounding landscapes. Visitors enamoured by these hobbit-style houses can indulge in a memorable stay at a trullo hotel or discover trullo churches that stand as intriguing testaments to the region's heritage. Additionally, the option of staying in the region's masserie, fortified farmhouses converted into boutique hotels or spa resorts, presents an opportunity to immerse oneself in the historical ambience of Valle d'Itria.

Exploring Valle d'Itria

Alberobello and its Trulli

Alberobello, a mesmerizing town in Puglia, boasts an enchanting collection of cone-shaped houses known as trulli, marking it as a UNESCO World Heritage Site. Strolling through the narrow streets of Alberobello, visitors are transported into a fairytale world, surrounded by the captivating whitewashed limestone structures that have graced this town for centuries.

The largest concentration of trulli in Alberobello can be found in two main areas: Rione Monti and Rione Aia Piccola. Notably, the Trullo Sovrano, situated at Piazza Sacramento, 10, 70011 Alberobello BA, Italy, stands as a must-visit attraction. This unique two-story trullo, serving as a museum, offers a glimpse into the past with its authentic furnishings dating back to the 18th century. Additionally, the Church of Sant'Antonio, also a trullo itself, presents a blend of history and architectural beauty.

Alberobello's well-signposted Rione Monti street leads tourists through a fairytale forest of around 1,500 trulli. Along this path, visitors encounter shops offering mini trulli, local crafts, olive oil, and delightful creamy liqueurs in a multitude of colours. The Church of Sant'Antonio, though relatively modern (dating from 1927), stands as a Trullo marvel worth exploring. For a more tranquil experience, the Rione Aia Piccola quarter on the eastern side offers a less touristy ambience, with many dwellings being family homes rather than dedicated to tourism.

Visitor Information

- Address: Trullo Sovrano, Piazza Sacramento, 10, 70011 Alberobello BA, Italy
- Hours of Operation: 10 am to 6 pm (Off-season: 10 am to 12:45 pm, 3:30 pm to 6 pm)

Martina Franca

Nestled in the heart of Puglia, Martina Franca stands tall as a top destination revered for its opulent Baroque architecture and cultural vibrancy. At its centrepiece lies the majestic Palazzo Ducale, located at Roma Square, Martina Franca, Taranto, 74015, an architectural marvel open to visitors from Monday to Sunday, 10:00 am to 1:00 pm, and from 4:00 pm to 7:00 pm, offering a glimpse into its historical grandeur. For further inquiries, contact them at 0833 262775. The allure of the town is heightened by its historic centre, known as Lama, situated at 23 Via Incrociata, Gallipoli, LE, 73014, inviting exploration with its intricate beauty and charm.

The charm of Martina Franca lies in its narrow streets adorned with elegant churches and graceful 18th-century townhouses, showcasing Baroque features and exquisite wrought-iron balconies. Visitors are captivated by the town's lively ambience, chic shops, and an array of gastronomic delights. The region's culinary prowess shines through its superb cold meats, cheeses, and pasta, accompanied by the local Martina Franca white wine, available in still or sparkling (Spumante) varieties.

Martina Franca's blend of architectural splendour, cultural festivals celebrating music and art, and its reputation for chic boutiques and gourmet delicacies make it a captivating destination within Valle d'Itria. The town's historical legacy, intertwined with its modern appeal, invites travellers to immerse themselves in its graceful streets, savour its culinary delights, and revel in the artistic ambience that defines this Baroque gem in Puglia.

Locorotondo

Nestled in the heart of Puglia, Locorotondo stands as a captivating destination celebrated for its circular layout and the enchanting sight of whitewashed houses adorned with vibrant flowers. As you meander through the labyrinthine alleys, the town unfolds panoramic views, creating a relaxed ambience in this hilltop gem.

Locorotondo's allure emanates from its historical centre situated at Via Federico II, 70010 - Locorotondo, Puglia, Italy. This core area invites exploration with its enduring beauty, providing visitors with a window into the region's abundant cultural heritage. For inquiries, contact them at 335 823 5203. Another must-visit attraction is the Chiesa di San Nicola di Myra, situated at Corso XX Settembre, Locorotondo, 70010, a place of spiritual and architectural significance.

Locorotondo, often overshadowed by its more famous neighbour Alberobello, offers a unique experience with its concentric circles of dazzling white houses. The neoclassical Chiesa di San Giorgio, with its vast dome and lofty bell tower, dominates the skyline, providing breathtaking views over the vineyards of the Itria Valley. Locorotondo is renowned for producing white, red, and rosé wines, with the white Locorotondo DOP being a local specialty.

Cisternino

Nestled on the edge of Valle d'Itria, Cisternino stands as a captivating destination renowned for its rustic beauty and traditional charm. The historic centre, located at 23 Via Incrociata, Gallipoli, LE, 73014, invites exploration, offering a glimpse into the town's historic essence. For inquiries, contact them at 345 215 3876. The iconic clock tower stands as a prominent landmark, adding to Cisternino's allure. At the same time, visitors can relish the authentic atmosphere, indulge in local cuisine, and bask in panoramic vistas over Valle d'Itria.

The Ponte della Madonnina, a pedestrian bridge, treats visitors to picturesque views of the lovely buildings surrounding it. For breathtaking views of the valley and local trulli, the Villa Comunale, a small urban park close to the Chiesa Matrice, offers an idyllic spot to soak in the scenery. The old quarter exudes an Asian-inspired appearance, with houses built around inner courtyards and outer staircases leading to upper floors.

Cisternino, known as "la città della bombetta" for its renowned meat delicacy, offers an array of family-run trattorias, highlighting the local bombetta—a savoury parcel of meat typically filled with cheese or spices and cooked on grills or in ovens. This quaint town beckons travellers to savour its culinary delights, bask in its picturesque landscapes and immerse themselves in its charming atmosphere rich with history and tradition.

Ostuni, the White City

Perched majestically on a hilltop, Ostuni, known as the White City, emerges as a premier destination in Puglia. Its striking, gleaming white buildings not only offer panoramic views of the Adriatic Sea but also weave a captivating fusion of ancient history and contemporary allure. Wandering through its winding alleys reveals a myriad of attractions, among which the Cathedral stands as a highlight. Located at [Exact Address Not Provided in the Article], the Cathedral boasts a remarkable and distinctive architectural style with concave and convex lines, featuring a stunning rose window adorned with 24 intricately carved sections symbolizing the hours of the day.

Ostuni's allure lies not only in its architectural marvels but also in the immersive experience of strolling through its labyrinthine streets, absorbing the captivating blend of ancient and modern elements. The town's gleaming white facades serve as a canvas for its rich history, offering visitors a glimpse into its cultural tapestry against the backdrop of breathtaking Adriatic Sea views. While specifics regarding operational hours, contact details, and admission fees for the Cathedral are not provided, exploring Ostuni promises an enchanting journey through a city that harmoniously intertwines its past and present.

Castellana Caves

The Castellana Caves, a natural wonder nestled in Puglia, stand as a premier destination celebrated for their mesmerizing stalactites and stalagmites. This underground labyrinth stretches across 3,348 meters and reaches a maximum depth of 122 meters below street level, showcasing an otherworldly landscape of stunning formations. Visitors are offered a unique opportunity to embark on guided tours through this subterranean marvel, immersing themselves in the ethereal beauty of the caves. Maintaining a constant temperature of approximately 16.5°C, these caves provide a comfortable and awe-inspiring experience for explorers seeking the wonders of nature.

The Castellana Caves offer a captivating journey through their labyrinthine passages adorned with intricate formations, allowing visitors to marvel at the sheer beauty and geological significance of stalactites and stalagmites. Although specific admission fees are not mentioned, the guided tours promise an enchanting exploration into an underground world filled with natural wonders. As visitors traverse the depths of these caves, they are treated to a surreal experience that showcases the marvels of nature hidden beneath the surface of Puglia.

Top Attractions & Activities
- Address: Anelli Square, Castellana Grotte, Bari, 70013
- Hours of Operation: Monday to Sunday, 10:00 am - 12:00 pm
- Contact Details: 080 499 8221

Olive Groves and Vineyards in Puglia

Puglia's Olive Groves and Vineyards, particularly nestled within the Valle d'Itria, offer immersive experiences that are essential for any visitor. This picturesque region is adorned with vast expanses of olive groves and lush vineyards, painting a mesmerizing landscape as far as the eye can behold. Visitors are invited to partake in olive oil tastings at local farms, delving into the intricate process of crafting olive oil while savouring its rich and diverse flavours. Exploring the vineyards stands as another highlight, providing an opportunity to taste the region's high-quality wines. Among the top vineyards to explore are I Pastini, L'Acropoli di Puglia, and Cantine Paololeo, each offering unique insights into Puglia's winemaking heritage.

Puglia's Olive Groves and Vineyards stand as an embodiment of the region's rich agricultural heritage. Visitors are encouraged to explore these scenic landscapes, engage in olive oil tastings, and delve into the world of winemaking, experiencing firsthand the flavours and craftsmanship that define Puglia's culinary identity.

5-Day Trip in Valle d'Itria

Day 1: Trulli Wonders and Olive Oil Delights

Morning: Embark on a 2-hour guided tour of Alberobello's iconic trulli, followed by a delightful breakfast at Trulli e Puglia Wine Bar.

Afternoon: Immerse yourself in local history with a History Walking Tour and Olive Oil Tasting. Continue to Locorotondo for a private tour and indulge in wine and local products tasting at a traditional winery.

Evening: Dine at Ristorante "Settetrulli" and take a stroll through the enchanting Trulli Zone.

Day 2: Martina Franca E-Bike Adventure and Culinary Delights

Morning: Enjoy an e-bike tour through the countryside, stopping for wine and bruschetta. Have breakfast at Pavì wine restaurant.

Afternoon: Explore Martina Franca on foot, indulge in a local cook's meal at Fasano Market Tour & Meal, and relax in the town's piazzas.

Evening: Dine at Michelin-starred Ristorante I Templari and take a passeggiata through Martina Franca's atmospheric streets.

Travel Tip: Bring sunscreen and a hat for the e-bike tour.

Day 3: The White City's History and Gastronomy

Morning: Take a private tour of Ostuni's historic centre and enjoy a traditional Apulian breakfast at Bel Sit.

Afternoon: Join an Olive Oil Tasting Tour and visit a winery in Cisternino for wine tasting. Explore the town of Cisternino.

Evening: Dine at Osteria La Valle and savour panoramic views.

Day 4: Seaside Serenity and City Highlights

Morning: Enjoy a private speedboat tour along the Monopoli coastline and breakfast at La Locanda del Macellaio.

Afternoon: Explore Monopoli's highlights on a walking tour, have lunch at Cibando, and relax on the beach or explore boutiques.

Evening: Dine at Il Trullo di Ninò and take a waterfront stroll.

Travel Tip: Bring a swimsuit and sunscreen for the boat tour.

Day 5: Fasano's Flavors and Countryside Charms

Morning: Experience Puglia Mozzarella at a local farm and have breakfast at Ristorante Torre di Angelucco.

Afternoon: Explore the countryside on an e-bike tour, stop at a Masseria for an olive oil tasting, and visit Ceglie Messapica.

Evening: Dine at Divino Wine Bar and savour the countryside tranquillity.

Travel Tip: Dress comfortably for the e-bike tour and farm visits.

CHAPTER 7

LOCAL CUISINES & DRINKS

CHAPTER 7

LOCAL CUISINES & DRINKS

Puglia's culinary scene offers a treasure trove of flavours deeply rooted in the tradition of cucina povera, emphasizing simple yet vibrant dishes. The region's cuisine celebrates fresh, locally sourced ingredients, showcasing the richness of its land and sea. A must-try is the pasta with chickpeas, embodying the essence of Puglian cooking—unpretentious yet profoundly satisfying. Another standout is the broad bean purée with wild chicory, highlighting the significance of seasonal produce and the region's commitment to freshness. Seafood lovers shouldn't miss the delectable mussels baked with potato and rice, an irresistible dish that captures the essence of Puglia's extensive coastline.

Puglia's healthy gastronomy revolves around vegetables, fruits, extra virgin olive oil, and durum wheat pasta, rich in protein and melatonin. With 60 million olive trees contributing significantly to Italy's olive oil exports and vineyards accounting for a substantial portion of the nation's wine production, the region's agricultural prowess is evident. Fresh seafood takes centre stage due to the region's expansive coastline, dominating menus with its abundance and variety. This culinary journey through Puglia promises a delightful fusion of simplicity, seasonality, and exceptional flavours, reflecting the region's culinary heritage and renaissance in transforming humble ingredients into fashionable and delectable dishes.

Orecchiette con Cime di Rape

Orecchiette con Cime di Rape stands as a hallmark dish of Puglia, encapsulating the region's rich culinary heritage and translating to "little ears with turnip tops," this dish centres around small ear-shaped pasta (orecchiette) harmoniously paired with broccoli rabe (cime di rapa), garlic cloves, red chilli, anchovies, and pecorino cheese. Its creation is a testament to Puglia's cucina povera, elevating humble ingredients into a flavorful ensemble.

This delightful dish can be found across Puglia, yet it's notably popular in Bari, where local artisans craft orecchiette by hand and sell it along the cobblestone streets. When dining out, such as at Ostuni Bistrot in Ostuni, expect an affordable price of around 12€ for a serving of Orecchiette con Cime di Rape.

Served hot, the plate arrives with perfectly cooked orecchiette coated in a light sauce derived from sautéed broccoli rabe, garlic, chilli, and anchovies. Often, a drizzle of olive oil and a sprinkle of pecorino cheese embellish this delectable creation. Anticipate robust and satisfying flavours that beautifully capture the freshness and quality of Puglia's locally sourced ingredients.

Pane di Altamura

Pane di Altamura stands as a cherished icon of Apulian culinary heritage, originating from the zone of Murgia Altamura in the province of Bari. This bread, revered for centuries, holds a prestigious place in Puglia's gastronomic culture. Crafted with ground semolina and 'grano duro' grain exclusively sourced from Alta Murgia, it's a blend of natural yeast, tepid water, and marine salt that forms its essence.

For the quintessential Pane di Altamura experience, Altamura itself, located west of Bari, boasts renowned bakeries like Porta Aurea and Panificio Non-Solo Pane - forno a legna. At an affordable price of one Euro per 1kg loaf, equivalent to approximately 1.30 USD, this world-famous bread, certified with DOP (Denominazione di Origine Protetta), promises an enduring freshness without preservatives.

Expect a sizable, round loaf with a robust crust and a soft, golden-hued interior when purchasing Pane di Altamura. Its exclusive use of semolina flour, derived from the "Senatore Cappelli" wheat variety, contributes to its distinct taste and texture. This flour, known for its nutty essence and golden hue, imparts a unique and unparalleled flavour profile to the bread.

Taralli

Taralli, emblematic of Puglia's culinary heritage, are small, crispy bread rings made from a dough enriched with oil. These traditional Italian snacks offer a delightful quick bite, resembling a savoury fusion between a bagel, pretzel, and breadstick. Crafted from simple ingredients such as all-purpose flour, fine sea salt, olive oil, and sometimes dry white wine or fennel seeds, Taralli capture the essence of Puglia's flavours in every bite.

Widely available across bakeries, pastry shops, and local restaurants, Taralli is commonly served alongside or instead of bread. Notable places to savour these savoury treats in Puglia include The Lady of Sweets and Panificio il Cugino in Molfetta. Offering affordability, the cost of Taralli varies but often ranges around €17.90, approximately $3, depending on size and flavour.

When indulging in Taralli, expect a small, savoury cracker meticulously shaped in a ring form. Their golden hue and crispy texture contribute to a unique taste that perfectly complements cheese boards, soups, or salads. They also make for a delightful appetizer, pairing exquisitely with a glass of robust red wine.

Antipasti

In Puglia, antipasti, or starters, serve as a flavorful introduction to the region's rich gastronomy, offering an assortment of local delicacies. This cherished culinary tradition presents an enticing medley of seafood, salumi (cold cuts), cheeses, and vegetables, setting the stage for an exquisite dining experience.

Antipasti in Puglia features a tempting array of offerings. The seafood-based antipasti di mare showcases delights like gamberoni (giant prawns), calamari (squid), vongole (clams), cozze (mussels), and polpo (octopus). Alternatively, assorted salumi platters highlight prosciutto crudo (dry-cured ham), salami, seasoned sausages, and bresaola, served alongside freshly baked bread and premium extra virgin olive oil. Vegetable antipasti often include pepperoni (peppers), zucchini (courgettes), melanzane (aubergine or eggplant), and 2carciofi (artichokes), reflecting the region's agricultural abundance.

Across Puglia, numerous restaurants offer delightful antipasti. Noteworthy spots to relish these starters include La Locanda dei Mercanti in Monopoli and Il Sorso Preferito in Bari. Antipasti in Puglia promises a culinary expedition, allowing you to sample a diverse range of local specialties. Opting for the antipasto misto (mixed starter) unveils a platter brimming with a dozen distinct dishes, offering a comprehensive tasting experience.

Caciocavallo

Caciocavallo, renowned for its distinctive shape and mild saltiness, stands as a prominent symbol of Apulian gastronomy. This traditional cheese, crafted from cow, ewe, or buffalo milk, embodies the essence of Puglia's culinary heritage.

Crafted from the milk of Podolian cows selected for their seasonal milk production, Caciocavallo undergoes a meticulous process. The curd, formed through heating and coagulation, is carefully heated again to achieve an elastic consistency, facilitating manipulation without breakage.

Cheese shops throughout Puglia offer this beloved cheese. Notable spots to savour Caciocavallo include Cime Di Tapas in Monopoli and select locales in the Gargano area. In Puglia, indulging in Caciocavallo is budget-friendly. A piece of this cheese typically costs around 17.90 euros.

When purchasing Caciocavallo in Puglia, anticipate a rounded cheese boasting a mild saltiness. The cheese's unique taste and texture derive from the exclusive use of Podolian cow's milk, offering a versatile snacking option or a delightful complement to various dishes.

Mozzarella, Burrata, and Stracciatella

The dairy legacy of Apulia extends beyond Caciocavallo, showcasing Mozzarella, Burrata, and Stracciatella as renowned local cheeses. These varieties epitomize the region's rich dairy heritage, offering a spectrum of flavours and textures that captivate cheese enthusiasts.

Crafted from fresh milk, Mozzarella undergoes stretching or pulling, whereas Burrata, a delectable delicacy, features a Mozzarella shell enfolding a creamy Stracciatella filling—fresh cream combined with bits of Mozzarella. Stracciatella itself is a soft, almost runny cheese, a blend of shredded Mozzarella curd and cream.

These cheeses grace the shelves of numerous cheese shops across Puglia. Prime spots to relish these delicacies include Cime Di Tapas in Monopoli, the Gargano area, and authentic dairy farms where these Apulian marvels are crafted. Indulging in Mozzarella, Burrata, and Stracciatella in Puglia is reasonably priced, with an approximate cost of 13.90 euros.

What to Expect: Embarking on a tasting journey of Mozzarella, Burrata, and Stracciatella unveils a diverse range of local specialties. Mozzarella presents as a solid, stretchy delight, Burrata reveals a solid exterior with an irresistibly creamy interior when sliced open, and Stracciatella showcases its soft, creamy texture—a cheese lover's dream.

Parmigiana di Melanzane

Parmigiana di Melanzane, also known as Eggplant Parmesan, stands as a celebrated culinary gem in Puglia. This dish embodies the region's rich gastronomic heritage, blending flavours that promise a delightful experience for any food enthusiast.

Thinly sliced eggplants take centre stage, fried to a golden hue, then meticulously layered with tomato sauce, Mozzarella cheese, and Parmesan cheese. The harmonious strata are baked to perfection, culminating in a hearty and flavoursome dish. Across Puglia, numerous restaurants offer Parmigiana di Melanzane. For an exceptional tasting experience, esteemed locales like Cime Di Tapas in Monopoli and the Gargano area beckon with their renditions of this dish.

Ordering Parmigiana di Melanzane unveils a culinary voyage, inviting a sampling of various local specialties. Served piping hot, the dish arrives with melted cheese and bubbling tomato sauce. Each bite reveals a tender and flavorful eggplant, saturated with the delectable essences of the sauce and cheese.

Il Primo

"Il Primo," or the first course in Puglia, often heralds the arrival of pasta, an esteemed staple of the region's culinary repertoire. Here, pasta is crafted from the simplest of ingredients—just flour and water—a tradition stemming from a time when eggs were a luxury beyond reach for the locals. This elemental preparation yields pasta that boasts delightful chewiness and inherent flavours, available in an array of shapes and sizes.

The region's hallmark pasta is the Orecchiette, aptly named "little ears," designed to cradle and complement various sauces. Most notably, it's often adorned with "cime di rapa," commonly translated as "turnip tops," but closer in resemblance to broccoli. Other pasta renditions enchant taste buds with combinations such as pomodori e ricotta forte (tomatoes and double-fermented ricotta), pomodori, cipolli e capocollo (cherry tomatoes, red onions, and diced capocollo), or the ever-comforting ragù di carne (meat sauce). Seafood pasta, adorned with fresh clams, calamari, prawns, lobster, or other oceanic treasures, abound as a delectable Puglian treat.

You'll find these pasta dishes gracing the menus of most restaurants scattered across Puglia. Eateries like Primo Restaurant in Lecce, Osteria Radici, and La Locanda di Ciacco stand out as excellent venues to relish these savoury delights.

Upon ordering Il Primo in Puglia, anticipate embarking on a gustatory expedition, relishing an assortment of local specialities. Each serving of pasta arrives steaming hot, impeccably coated in its sauce, ensuring a symphony of flavours that speak volumes about the freshness and quality of the region's ingredients.

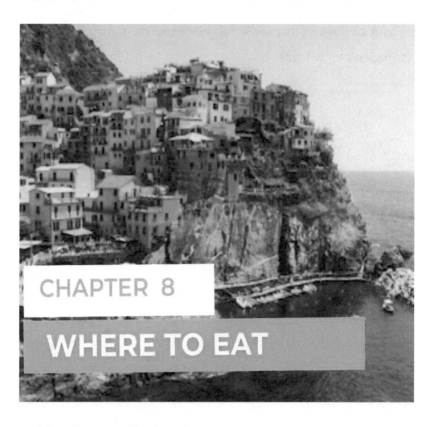

CHAPTER 8

WHERE TO EAT

CHAPTER 8

WHERE TO EAT

Main meals in Puglia often find their place in ristorantes, trattorias, or osterias. The distinctions between these establishments have blurred over time. What was once a traditional osteria—a haven for wine and pasta—now spans the spectrum from classic to trendy, offering an evolving dining experience.

Puglia's pizzerias tantalize with offerings beyond just pizza, often featuring pasta and meat dishes. The finest among them serve pizzas straight from wood-fired brick ovens, delivering that perfect bubbling crust. Evening is the favored time for pizza indulgence, often paired with beer instead of wine. Grab-and-go pizza al taglio, sold by the slice, is a local favorite for quick takeaways.

For a swift bite, navigate towards a bar or café showcasing an assortment of rolls and sandwiches. Opting to stand at the bar (al banco) proves more economical compared to seated service.

Wine aficionados, look no further than an enoteca—a refined wine bar boasting an impressive selection available by the glass. These establishments often provide optional platters of cheese or cold meats, perfectly complementing their curated wine offerings.

Price Range
Dining costs in Puglia can vary, offering options for various budgets:
€€€€: Over 50 euros
€€€: 35–50 euros
€€: 25–35 euros
€: Below 25 euros

The Gargano Peninsula

Vieste Restaurants

Vieste, nestled within the picturesque Gargano Peninsula, is renowned for its delectable seafood and authentic Italian gastronomy. Here are some of the standout dining establishments:

Caffè Del Mare: Found at Corso Fazzini, Vieste, this restaurant welcomes patrons daily from 06:00 to 00:00, offering a delightful culinary experience.

Ristorante Osteria Pane & Vino: Situated at Strada Statale 89 km. 87, 5 direzione Vieste del Gargano, Peschici, 710103; this eatery serves guests from 12:30 to 14:30 and 19:00 to 23:00 on weekdays, extending its hours from 12:30 to 23:00 on weekends. Reach them at 377 594 78993.

La Masseria: Located at Sp 52 km 8, 7 Litoranea Vieste - Peschici, Vieste, 710194, this restaurant opens its doors from 19:30 to 00:00 daily. Contact them at 388 355 15274.

Pelikano Ristorante: Positioned at Lungomare Enrico Mattei 9 B, Vieste, 710195, this dining spot offers its services from 12:30 to 14:30 and 19:30 to 22:30 daily. Contact them at 0884 7024895.

Price Range: The average cost per person in these esteemed restaurants falls between €€ to €€€.

Peschici Restaurants

Peschici, nestled within the stunning Gargano Peninsula, boasts a diverse array of dining establishments catering to varied tastes and preferences. Here are some of the noteworthy restaurants in Peschici:

Il Trabucco: Found at Località Punta San Nicola, Peschici, 710102, this restaurant welcomes guests daily from 12:30 to 15:00 and 19:00 to 22:00.

Casa Vacanze La Cantinetta: Situated at Viale Kennedy, 71, 71010 - Peschici, this restaurant extends its services daily from 12:00 to 15:00 and 19:00 to 23:20.

Al Trabucco Da Mimì: Located at Località Punta San Nicola, Peschici, 710104, this eatery greets visitors every day from 11:30 to 14:30 and 18:30 to 22:00. Contact them at 0884 962556.

Ristorante Osteria Pane & Vino: Positioned at Strada Statale 89 km. 87, 5 direzione Vieste del Gargano, Peschici, 710105; this restaurant serves patrons from 12:30 to 15:00 and 19:30 to 23:00 on weekdays, extending its hours from 12:30 to 23:00 on weekends. Reach them at 377 594 7899.

Price Range: The approximate cost per person across these esteemed dining spots generally falls within the € to €€ range.

San Giovanni Rotondo Restaurants

Nestled within the picturesque Gargano Peninsula, San Giovanni Rotondo beckons with its diverse culinary landscape, offering a fusion of local flavors and international cuisines. Here are some standout dining venues in San Giovanni Rotondo:

Ristorante al Cavallino Rosso: Discover this gem at Via Tratturo delle Corse,14, 71013, San Giovanni Rotondo. Operating hours span from

12:30 to 15:00 and 19:00 to 22:00 daily. Contact: 0884 962556. Average cost per person: €26.

Ristorante Vineria Sale e Pepe: Indulge in gastronomic delights at Viale Aldo Moro, 125, 71013, San Giovanni Rotondo. Open daily from 12:30 to 15:00 and 19:00 to 22:00. Average price per person: €27.

Osteria Antica Piazzetta: Savor delectable dishes at Viale Aldo Moro 161, 71013, San Giovanni Rotondo. Operating hours: 12:30 to 15:00 and 19:00 to 22:00 daily. Average cost per person: €30.

San Giovanni Rotondo Restaurants

San Giovanni Rotondo, nestled in the picturesque Gargano Peninsula, features a charming collection of restaurants that serve a mix of local specialties and international cuisine. Here are some of the prominent dining venues in San Giovanni Rotondo:

Ristorante al Cavallino Rosso: Find this culinary gem at Via Tratturo delle Corse,14, 71013, San Giovanni Rotondo. Open daily from 12:00 to 15:00 and 19:00 to 22:00. Contact: 0884 962556. Average cost per person: €22.

Ristorante Vineria Sale e Pepe: Delight in a dining experience at Viale Aldo Moro, 125, 71013, San Giovanni Rotondo. Operating hours: 12:30 to 15:00 and 19:00 to 22:00 daily. Average price per person: €25.

Osteria Antica Piazzetta: Enjoy culinary delights at Viale Aldo Moro 161, 71013, San Giovanni Rotondo. Open daily from 12:30 to 15:00 and 19:00 to 22:00. Average cost per person: €23.

Mattinata Restaurants

In Mattinata, a charming town nestled within the Gargano Peninsula, visitors can explore a diverse culinary scene offering traditional Italian fare and delightful pizzerias. Here are some noteworthy restaurants:

- **Scarpetta D'Oro**: Known for its Italian, Pizza, Seafood, and Mediterranean dishes.
- **Lido Cala Rosa:** Offers a diverse menu featuring Italian, Seafood, and Mediterranean cuisine.
- **B&B Dalla Nonna:** Renowned for its local cuisine.

While specific pricing details aren't provided, these establishments offer a range of prices from moderate to mid-range. Unfortunately, detailed contact information, opening hours, and precise pricing per person are not available in the provided content.

Puglia Imperiale

Casa Sgarra stands as a renowned seafront restaurant in Trani, offering an exquisite blend of traditional Puglian flavors infused with a modern culinary touch. Known for its warm hospitality and exceptional cuisine, Casa Sgarra presents a delightful dining experience.

Contact Details:

- Address: Lungomare C. Colombo, 114, Trani, 761252
- Phone: +39 349 186 7499
- Website: www.casasgarra.it
- Opening Hours: Monday, Wednesday, Thursday, Friday, Saturday, Sunday: 13:00 - 15:00, 20:00 - 23:30. Closed on Tuesdays

In Lecce, **Bros Restaurant** stands out as a culinary gem, offering an innovative and contemporary dining experience. Renowned for its creative surprises like the "Fucking Cold Egg" or the "Spaghetti timbale," this establishment presents a menu that delights in unexpected and theatrical culinary presentations.

Contact Details:

- Address: Via degli Acaja 2, Lecce, 731002
- Phone: +39 351 661 5513
- Website: www.brosrestaurant.it
- Opening Hours: Wednesday to Sunday: 12:00 PM - 1:00 PM, 8:00 PM - 9:00 PM. Closed on Monday and Tuesday

In the heart of Putignano Bari lies **Angelo Sabatelli**, a culinary gem that masterfully blends the essence of local produce with innovative twists, occasionally incorporating Asian influences. Nestled within the historic center, this restaurant exudes elegance through contemporary dining spaces, providing the perfect backdrop for the technically crafted cuisine curated by a talented and visionary chef. Angelo Sabatelli offers an exploration of flavors where the richness of local ingredients takes center stage, enhanced by intriguing hints of Asian influence.

Contact Details:
- Address: Via Santa Chiara 1, Putignano, 700172
- Phone: +39 080 405 2733
- Website: www.angelosabatelliristorante.com
- Opening Hours: Tuesday to Sunday: 12:30 PM - 2:00 PM, 7:30 PM - 10:00 PM. Closed on Monday.

Bari

Situated at Corso Vittorio Emanuele II, 13, 70122 Bari BA, Italy, **Ristorante Biancofiore** beckons with a captivating seafront dining experience. This esteemed establishment is renowned for its ingenious blend of traditional Puglian flavors infused with a contemporary touch, ensuring a unique culinary journey for visitors. The menu boasts an array of innovative and surprising tasting dishes, often presented with a theatrical flair right at your table, elevating the dining experience.

Contact Details:
- Address: Corso Vittorio Emanuele II 13, Bari, 70122
- Phone: +39 080 523 5446
- Website: www.ristorantebiancofiore.it
- Opening Hours: Monday to Sunday: 12:30 PM - 2:30 PM, 7:00 PM - 10:30 PM. Closed on Tuesday

Nestled at Corso Vittorio Emanuele II 15, Bari, 701221, **Mastro Ciccio** stands as a beloved culinary spot offering an enticing array of Italian delights. From savory pasta dishes to delectable sandwiches, meatballs, and the renowned panzerotto, this eatery caters to diverse tastes. Praised for its dedication to quality ingredients and its emphasis on showcasing local flavors, Mastro Ciccio crafts handcrafted sandwiches using 100% Pugliese semolina, embodying the essence of the region's gastronomy. With an approximate price range per person between €3 and €16, this establishment invites patrons to relish authentic Italian flavors without breaking the bank. Operating from 10:00 AM to 12:00 AM, Mastro Ciccio warmly welcomes visitors to savor its culinary offerings. For further inquiries, feel free to reach out at +39 080 521 0001.

Situated at Via Putignani, 213/215, Bari, 701221, **Terranima** beckons visitors with its delightful array of Italian culinary delights, encompassing local cuisine, Mediterranean flavors, and irresistible street food. This charming restaurant exudes a vibrant ambiance, complemented by its warm and hospitable staff, offering an authentic taste of Pugliese cuisine. With an approximate price range per person spanning from €10 to €30, patrons can indulge in a diverse menu without straining their wallets. Terranima extends its welcome from 12:00 PM to 3:30 PM and 7:00 PM to 11:30 PM, Monday through Saturday, and from 12:00 PM to 4:00 PM on Sundays. For further details or reservations, reach out at +39 080 521 9725 or explore their offerings at https://www.terranima.com/.

Situated at Via Leopardi 38, Torre a Mare, Bari, 701261, **Ristorante Giannino** stands as a renowned culinary destination offering an exquisite blend of Italian delicacies and tantalizing seafood dishes. With its emphasis on authentic Apulian cuisine and a captivating ambiance, this restaurant crafts a unique dining experience. The approximate price range per person spans from €49 to €147, reflecting the diverse and upscale menu. Operating hours are from 12:30 PM to 3:00 PM and 8:00 PM to 10:30 PM, Monday to Saturday, and from 12:30 PM to 3:00 PM on Sundays. For inquiries or reservations, contact Ristorante Giannino at +39 080 543 0448 or explore further details on their website: http://www.ristorantegiannino.com/.

Situated at Via Giovanni Amendola 203, 70126, Bari, Italy, **Hagakure - Fusion e Sushi** is a highly acclaimed restaurant offering a diverse array of Japanese, seafood, sushi, and Asian cuisine. Renowned for its blend of traditional and fusion dishes, the restaurant prides itself on delivering flavorful and fresh meals. The approximate price range per person spans from €22 to €38, catering to various preferences and tastes. Operating details include contact via +39 080 548 4792 for further inquiries.

Valle d'Itria

Located at via Valle d'Itria 96, Rotonda via Locorotondo, Martina Franca, 740151, **Pizza Divina** stands as a highly acclaimed restaurant in Valle d'Itria. This top-rated establishment offers a diverse range of Italian, pizza, Mediterranean, and European cuisines, showcasing high-quality traditional dishes in a welcoming and friendly atmosphere. The approximate price range per person falls between €7 and €12. Operating from 7:30 PM to 2:00 AM every day, Pizza Divina ensures a delightful culinary experience. For additional details, inquiries can be made via phone at +39 347 862 3806 or by visiting their website: https://www.pizzadivinamartinafranca.it/

Nestled at Via Valle d'Itria 95, Svincolo per Cisternino, Martina Franca, 740151, **Divino Wine & Food** stands as a distinguished restaurant in Valle d'Itria. This top-rated establishment offers a delightful array of Italian, Mediterranean, and vegetarian-friendly dishes, highlighting its commitment to quality cuisine. With an approximate price range per person spanning between €16 and €47, the restaurant ensures a premium culinary experience. Open daily from 12:35 PM to 12:30 AM, Divino Wine & Food provides an elegant atmosphere complemented by a friendly staff. For further details or reservations, inquiries can be made by contacting +39 329 312 9325 or by visiting their website: https://divinovineria.it/

Evo Ristorante, situated at Via Papa Giovanni XXIII 1, Presso Trullo Sovrano/Piazza Sacramento 14, Alberobello, 700111, stands as a culinary gem in Valle d'Itria. This esteemed restaurant has earned its top-rated status by offering a diverse menu featuring Italian, seafood, Mediterranean, and European cuisines. The enchanting setting includes a delightful garden, creating an inviting atmosphere for patrons. Known for its commitment to showcasing the finest ingredients from Puglia, Evo Ristorante presents complex and elaborate dishes. With a price range per

151

person spanning approximately €44 to €88, the restaurant guarantees a premium dining experience. Operating hours are from 19:00 to 23:00 on Monday and Tuesday, 12:00 to 23:00 on Friday, 11:59 to 15:30, 19:20 to 22:00 on Saturday, and 12:30 to 15:30 on Sunday. For reservations or further inquiries, feel free to contact them at +39 320 848 1230 or visit their website: https://www.evoristorante.com/

Salento

Osteria Sant'Anna, nestled at Viale Stazione 12, Cisternino, 720141, stands as a celebrated dining establishment in Valle d'Itria. Renowned for its top-rated status, this restaurant offers a diverse array of Italian, Mediterranean, and vegetarian-friendly dishes. What sets this place apart is its captivating ambiance, featuring soulful house settings, striking star vaults, and walls adorned with the history and craftsmanship of years gone by. The refined atmosphere, complemented by period furniture, creates an inviting and unique dining experience. The price range per person spans approximately €30 to €50, promising an exceptional culinary journey. Operating hours are from 12:00 to 14:00 and 20:00 to 23:00 from Tuesday to Sunday. For further details or reservations, please get in touch with them at +39 080 444 7036 or visit their website: https://osteriasantanna.it/

Cumaná Bistro Food, situated at Carrera 4 Con Calle 4 3-55, Salento, Quindío Department, 6310201, stands as one of the prominent dining spots in Salento. This top-rated restaurant offers a diverse menu featuring Italian, Mediterranean, and European cuisines, providing a wide array of flavors and culinary experiences. Renowned for its high-quality cuisine, the restaurant prides itself on its delightful dishes, complemented by a welcoming and gracious staff in an elegant atmosphere. The price range per person is approximately €7 - €17, making it accessible to various budgets. Operating hours vary: they're open from 14:00 to 20:00 on Monday, 12:30 to 16:30 on Tuesday, 14:00 to 20:00 from Thursday to Saturday, and 12:30 to 20:00 on Sunday. For additional information or reservations, feel free to contact them at +39 316 30021421 or visit their website: https://cumanabistrofood.com/

Basilicata

Pizzeria La Macina stands as a top-rated dining spot at Via Brindisi Fiore 38, Rionero In Vulture, 850281, in the heart of Basilicata. This esteemed eatery presents an extensive menu blending Italian, pizza, Mediterranean, and European cuisines, ensuring a wide array of flavors to satisfy different preferences. Its reputation is built upon serving high-quality traditional dishes in a warm and inviting atmosphere. The price range per person is approximately €7 - €17, making it an affordable yet delightful dining option. Operating hours are from 18:30 to 00:00, welcoming guests throughout the evenings from Monday to Saturday. For further details or reservations, you can reach out to them at +39 0972 080348.

Nestled in Via Bruno Buozzi 11, Matera, **L'Abbondanza Lucana** specializes in serving delectable Lucanian cuisine, highlighting local cheeses and meats as appetizers, and featuring robust pasta dishes with fava beans, mixed vegetables, and mint as main courses. The restaurant occupies a series of caves with an outdoor area, offering a unique dining experience in the heart of the old town. Known for its substantial portions, especially the antipasti, it impresses diners with its thoughtfully curated local dishes and ingredients.

- Address: Via Bruno Buozzi 11, Matera, 751001
- Phone: +39 0835 334574
- Opening Hours: 7:30 PM to 1 AM (Tue to Thu), 12 PM to 3 PM & 7 PM to 1 AM (Fri), 7 PM to 2 AM (Sat), 12 PM to 4 PM (Sun)
- Price Range: Approximately €38 - €54 per person

Baccanti stands as a top-rated restaurant nestled in Basilicata, Puglia, offering a diverse array of culinary delights spanning Italian, Mediterranean, and European cuisines. Known for its commitment to high-quality traditional fare and fostering a welcoming atmosphere, Baccanti entices diners with its rich flavors and friendly ambiance. The price range per person falls approximately between €8 to €21.

San Barbato Resort Spa & Golf is a distinguished 5-star establishment situated at S.S. 93, Km 53,300 – 85024 Lavello (P.Z.) in Basilicata, Italy. Renowned for its exceptional dining experience, the resort boasts a restaurant offering a blend of Italian, Mediterranean, and International cuisines. Guests are drawn to the world-class amenities, including exemplary service, a well-equipped fitness center, complimentary private parking, lush gardens, and a scenic terrace. The average price range per person falls between €50 to €100. For precise opening hours, it's recommended to refer to their website: https://sanbarbatoresort.com/. For inquiries or reservations, contact them at +39 0972 816011.

CHAPTER 9

WHERE TO STAY

Bari

Gargano

Valle d'Itria

Salento

CHAPTER 9

WHERE TO STAY

P uglia beckons travelers with an extensive spectrum of lodging choices, ensuring a perfect match for every preference and pocket. Whether you seek the indulgence of opulent five-star hotels, the enchanting allure of converted farmhouses known as masserie, trendy boutique hotels, distinctive trulli accommodations, unassuming guest houses, budget-friendly hostels, convenient apartments, or the personalized comfort of Airbnbs, Puglia boasts a diverse array of options tailored to cater to every traveler's desires.

During the high season from Easter through to September, and especially in July and August, it's wise to book ahead, particularly for popular coastal resorts. Off-season, you'll often find rates dramatically reduced. Some hotels may insist on a minimum stay during the high season, and many of the recommended accommodations, particularly the masserie, are pretty rural, so having a car would be beneficial.

It's also important to note the Tourist Tax (Tassa di Soggiorno), which must be paid directly by tourists during their stay. The costs range from €1–6 per person per night, up to a maximum of five (or sometimes three) consecutive overnight stays. The rate varies according to the type of accommodation, and children under 12–14 (the age varies) are exempt from the charge or pay a discounted rate.

The symbols below provide a rough indication of rates per night for a double room with a bathroom in high season, including breakfast but excluding tourist tax:

€€€€: over 350 euros

€€€: 200–350 euros

€€: 120–200 euros

€: less than 120 euros

Bari

Hotel Boston

Hotel Boston presents itself as a reputable lodging choice situated in Bari's heart, Italy. The hotel provides air-conditioned rooms featuring complimentary Wi-Fi access and a generous breakfast buffet. A night's stay typically costs around €68, equivalent to approximately $76. For inquiries or bookings, contact them at +39 080 521 6633. You can find Hotel Boston at Via Piccinni 155, Bari, Puglia, 70122. Delving into simplicity without compromising comfort, the rooms are adorned with essential furnishings, each equipped with a TV and minibar. The private bathrooms boast either a bath or shower, alongside provided amenities like a hairdryer. Strategically located, the hotel offers proximity to Bari's historic center and St. Nicholas's Cathedral, within a short stroll, and easy access to the shopping district of Via Sparano. With a 24-hour reception, the attentive staff caters to guests' needs round the clock, ensuring a pleasant stay.

The Nicolaus Hotel

The Nicolaus Hotel stands as an esteemed accommodation choice nestled in Bari, Italy. This distinguished hotel presents stylish rooms paired with complimentary Wi-Fi, setting the stage for a comfortable stay. With a fully equipped wellness area comprising an indoor pool, gym, sauna, Turkish bath, and hot tub, guests can unwind in absolute luxury. The price for a night's stay hovers around €267, approximately $300. For reservations or inquiries, reach out to +39 080 568 2555. You'll find the Nicolaus Hotel situated at Via Cardinal A. Ciasca 9, Bari, 70124. Renowned for its modern design and non-smoking rooms, each accommodation is equipped with air conditioning and a TV featuring satellite and pay-per-view channels. Most spaces also boast a balcony, offering a serene spot to unwind. Adding to the allure, THE SEASONS restaurant, an à la carte dining option within the hotel, specializes in an enticing blend of Italian and Puglia specialties. Additionally, guests benefit from a complimentary scheduled shuttle service to Bari Airport. For further details, explore their website.

JR Hotels Oriente Bari

JR Hotels Oriente Bari stands as a sought-after accommodation in Bari, Italy, offering a comfortable retreat for travelers. Each room is equipped with air conditioning, a flat-screen satellite TV, and a minibar, ensuring a cozy stay. The price per night for this experience is approximately €92, equivalent to about $103. For inquiries or reservations, contact +39 080 525 5100. You'll find the hotel at Corso Cavour 32, Bari, 70122. Set within a wholly renovated early 20th-century building, the hotel boasts a 24-hour reception ready to assist with car rentals, while Wi-Fi is accessible throughout the property. Each room features a private bathroom with a shower and bathrobe, ensuring comfort and convenience during your stay. Guests can unwind at the hotel's bar, offering snacks and drinks, or enjoy the scenic rooftop terrace with panoramic views of Bari. With the city's historic center and seafront promenade merely a 5-minute walk away and Bari's Central Station situated 750 meters from the hotel, JR Hotels Oriente Bari offers both comfort and convenience for travelers seeking a delightful stay in Bari.

Hotel Pensione Romeo

Hotel Pensione Romeo, a well-liked budget-friendly option in Bari, Italy, offers classic-style rooms with complimentary Wi-Fi, providing a comfortable stay for travelers. The approximate price per night is around £47, equivalent to approximately $63. For inquiries or bookings, you can contact the hotel at +39 080 523 7253. Find the hotel at Via Scipione Crisanzio 12, Bari, 70122. Situated within a convenient 5-minute walk from Bari Centrale Train Station, this hotel provides easy access for travelers. The rooms are furnished with a TV and feature fully equipped en suite bathrooms. Bari Cathedral, a significant landmark, is merely 1 km away, while the harbor can be reached with a pleasant 12-minute stroll. The hotel boasts a 24-hour front desk and complimentary Wi-Fi access, ensuring guests can stay connected throughout their stay. For guests arriving by car, paid public parking is available nearby.

Trulli Terra Magica

Trulli Terra Magica, a sought-after budget hotel nestled in Putignano, Bari, Italy, offers cozy rooms, some housed in traditional Trulli, the iconic Apulian stone houses. With an approximate price of £60 per night, roughly equivalent to $80, the hotel provides a serene retreat. For reservations or inquiries, contact the hotel at +39 345 501 1225. Find the hotel at Strada Comunale San Cataldo,12, Putignano, 70017. Surrounded by its lush garden, this hotel boasts complimentary Wi-Fi throughout the premises and free private parking for guests. Indulge in a delightful breakfast spread before setting out to explore the area. The accommodations showcase an elegant rustic design, complete with amenities like a flat-screen TV with satellite channels, a minibar, and an en suite bathroom stocked with toiletries. All rooms offer serene garden views. With Monopoli's stunning beaches just a 30-minute drive away, and Putignano Train Station a mere 2 km from the hotel, guests have convenient access to nearby attractions. Additionally, Bari Airport is approximately an hour's drive away. Visit Trulli Terra Magica's website for more detailed information and bookings.

Gargano

Hotel Torre Santamaria Resort in Gargano, Puglia:
- Hotel Name: Hotel Torre Santamaria Resort
- Physical Address: Contrada Funni, 25, Mattinata, Puglia, 71030
- Price Range: €€

Nestled in the serene landscape of Mattinata in Puglia, Hotel Torre Santamaria Resort offers a delightful retreat accentuated by its picturesque garden setting. Renowned for its inviting poolside breakfast amidst a charming garden ambiance, this top-rated hotel presents an array of comfortable accommodations. Each unit is thoughtfully furnished with modern amenities like a flat-screen TV, air conditioning, and bathrooms equipped with showers and hairdryers. Guests can relish the serene surroundings from their private patio with delightful garden views. With an attentive and accommodating staff, this resort promises a tranquil and enjoyable stay, perfect for those seeking a peaceful haven amidst nature's beauty.

Hotel Centro di Spiritualità Padre Pio

- Physical Address: Via Anna Frank, San Giovanni Rotondo, 710131
- Contact Number: [Contact Information Not Provided]
- Price Range: €€€

Hotel Centro di Spiritualità Padre Pio, a distinguished 4-star hotel nestled on Via Anna Frank in San Giovanni Rotondo, offers a tranquil retreat mere minutes away from the revered Padre Pio Sanctuary. This top-rated establishment prides itself on its exceptional location and unparalleled customer service. The hotel offers various amenities, such as a restaurant serving delightful cuisine, a spiritual center with two chapels, and a generous convention hall. Each room, equipped with modern conveniences like air conditioning, satellite TV, and complimentary Wi-Fi, provides a comfortable and serene environment. Whether seeking spiritual solace or simply exploring the region, this hotel promises a peaceful stay with its dedication to service and convenient proximity to the Padre Pio Sanctuary.

Casapaceebene is a highly-rated 2-star hotel situated at Corso Roma 83, San Giovanni Rotondo, 710131. Guests can enjoy the convenience of shared lounge facilities and complimentary private parking during their stay. This hotel offers air-conditioned rooms equipped with complimentary Wi-Fi, ensuring guests stay connected throughout. Each room features a private bathroom, a desk, and a wardrobe, providing comfort and functionality for a relaxing stay. Price Range: €

Hotel Puglia Garden stands as a highly-rated 4-star retreat located at Localita Macchia di Mauro, 71019, Vieste, Italy. Nestled amid the lush greenery of olive and orange groves, this hotel provides an array of amenities ensuring a memorable stay. Guests can expect a dedicated concierge service, 24-hour front desk assistance, and convenient ticketing services. Situated a mere 5 minutes from Vieste's golden sandy beaches and city center, the hotel offers spacious air-conditioned rooms, both indoor and outdoor swimming pools, and a convenient shuttle service to their partnered beach. Additionally, guests enjoy the added perks of complimentary parking and free Wi-Fi across all areas. For further details or reservations, you can reach Hotel Puglia Garden at +39 08845953693 or visit their website at https://www.hotelpugliagarden.it/en/. Price Range: €€€

Forte 2 Hotel, situated in Vieste, stands as a top-rated accommodation renowned for its exceptional staff and diverse breakfast offerings. This hotel presents a delightful ambiance with a well-tended garden, a seasonal outdoor swimming pool, and comfortably appointed air-conditioned rooms equipped with complimentary WiFi, offering guests splendid views of the sea. While the specific price range per night in euros is not outlined, you can gather further details or make reservations by contacting them directly via their phone number or by visiting their website at https://www.forte2hotel.com/. Price Range: €€

La Chiusa delle More stands as a tranquil country hotel nestled in the scenic landscape, located around 1.5 kilometers (1 mile) west of Peschici in the Gargano region. Resting on a hillside amidst an ancient olive grove and just a kilometer (half a mile) from the coast, this hotel was artfully transformed from an old farmhouse. Celebrated for its exceptional culinary offerings and welcoming hosts, it also offers cookery courses during specific months in May, June, and September. The price range per night typically falls between €200 to €350 in euros, which translates to approximately $220 to $385 in dollars. La Chiusa delle More operates from late May to the end of September, providing an ideal retreat. For further inquiries or reservations, you can reach them at +39 330 543 7661 or explore their offerings on their website at https://www.lachiusadellemore.it/.

Hotel Seggio is a welcoming, family-operated three-star establishment situated at Via Vesta, 7 in Vieste. Positioned in the heart of the historic town, perched atop the cliffs, it offers splendid panoramic views of the sea. With 22 well-appointed rooms, this hotel provides its guests with a small pool and access to a petite beach area via a convenient lift. Although there isn't on-site parking, the attentive staff is always on hand to help guests find suitable parking spaces and assist with luggage. The price range per night typically falls between €50 to €200 in euros, equivalent to approximately $55 to $220 in dollars. For further inquiries or bookings, you can reach out to them at +39 0884 708123 or explore more about their offerings on their website at https://hotelseggio.it/.

Valle d'Itria

La Peschiera stands as a luxurious 5-star haven perched on the Adriatic Sea in Monopoli, Puglia, offering an exclusive retreat along the region's picturesque shores. The hotel, located at Contrada Losciale 63, Savelletri Di Fasano, 700431, can be reached at +39 080 8015991, and more details can be found on their website: https://www.peschierahotel.com/. Indulge in the culinary delights at the hotel's restaurant, Sale Blu, renowned for its fresh seafood dishes. The menu offers an array of options suitable for daytime snacks, lighter meals, or evening delicacies, ensuring there's something to satisfy every palate. Additionally, La Peschiera is conveniently close to Sabbiadoro Beach, Alborada S.a.s, and Lido Marina Grande—enticing attractions for those seeking a day of relaxation and exploration.

Truddhi Casa e Cucina di Puglia
- Address: S.P.226 Contrada Trito 161, Locorotondo, 700101
- Phone: +39 340 4130855
- Website: Truddhi Casa e Cucina di Puglia

Nestled in the serene Itria Valley near Locorotondo, Truddhi Casa e Cucina di Puglia offers a unique stay in traditional Trulli stone houses, surrounded by vineyards and olive groves. The accommodations are equipped with kitchenettes featuring essential appliances like a microwave, electric kettle, and toaster, while the garden area provides barbecue facilities. The property enjoys a tranquil ambience and is a brief 7-minute drive away from local restaurants and cafés.

Attraction-wise, the UNESCO World Heritage Site at Alberobello, famed for its Trulli structures, is a mere 12 km away. For those seeking a beach escape, the Adriatic's sandy shores are a convenient 20-minute drive by car. Moreover, guests have easy access to a nearby mini-market, just a 2-minute walk from the property. The location offers a peaceful rural retreat with proximity to both cultural landmarks and natural beauty.

Masseria San Domenico

- Address: Strada Provinciale 90 3, 72015 Savelletri di Fasano, Brindisi, Italy
- Phone: +39 080 4827769
- Website: https://www.masseriasandomenico.com/en/

Masseria San Domenico stands as a luxurious 5-star resort, showcasing a historic 14th-century fortified farmhouse that once served as a watchtower for the Knights of Malta. Transformed into a deluxe boutique-style resort, it offers an intimate and opulent stay alongside top-tier facilities.

The resort's gastronomic experience is a delight, boasting three luxurious restaurants that showcase traditional recipes crafted from fresh, locally sourced ingredients and home-grown vegetables. Indulge in authentic flavours and excellent wines that encapsulate the essence of Puglia.

Adjacent attractions include Zoosafari and Torre Canne Beach, both within a convenient 10-minute drive from the resort. For those seeking leisurely outdoor activities, an 18-hole golf course overlooking the Adriatic Sea awaits golf enthusiasts, promising a delightful experience amidst stunning vistas.

Masseria Il Frantoio

- Address: S.S. 16 Km 874, Ostuni, 72017
- Phone: +39 0831 330276
- Website: Masseria Il Frantoio
- Opening Hours: 10:00 AM - 2:30 PM | 8:30 PM - 10:30 PM (Monday to Sunday)

Nestled in the serene Puglian countryside, Masseria Il Frantoio stands as an alluring and esteemed farmhouse retreat located just a stone's throw away from the charming town of Ostuni. This organic farm, steeped in history as one of the original masserie, offers a truly immersive experience into the rich culinary traditions of Puglia.

Experience the essence of the region's gastronomy through communal settings offering eight-, six--, or four-course organic lunches or dinners.

Here, guests delight in the finest cuisine created from locally sourced, fresh ingredients and the farm's exceptional olive oil. The menu dynamically evolves with the seasons, incorporating the daily bounty of Puglia. Delights from their citrus grove, such as pear, orange, and tangerine jams, grace the tables. The fragrant durum wheat yields the region's characteristic bread and diverse pasta varieties.

Surrounded by historical marvels like Masseria Brancati, a captivating museum, and the natural splendour of Valle d'Itria e Dintorni, guests at Masseria Il Frantoio are also a mere 5 kilometres (3 miles) away from the captivating Adriatic Sea.

Salento

Centro Storico B&B

- Address: Via Andrea Vignes 2, 73100, Lecce, Italy
- Phone: +39 083 2242 727
- website: http://www.centrostoricolecce.it/

Centro Storico B&B is a charming accommodation nestled in the historic Palazzo Astore, conveniently located just a short stroll away from Lecce's main monuments. The rooms are equipped with tea and coffee-making facilities. Guests are provided with vouchers for breakfast at a nearby café, ensuring a delightful start to the day. The Duomo Suite, situated at the top with its private terrace, offers the finest experience, although please note that there's no lift available at the B&B. The B&B is in proximity to Museo Faggiano, an intriguing history museum, and Piazza del Duomo, a historic area perfect for leisurely walks and exploring the city's heritage.

Masseria Sant'Angelo Agriturismo

- Address: Case Sparse Sant'Angelo, Corigliano d'Otranto
- Phone: +39 0836 320575
- Website: https://www.masseriasantangelo.it/en/

Masseria Sant'Angelo Agriturismo is an authentic family-operated working farm located in Corigliano d'Otranto, Salento. The agriturismo offers a genuine experience steeped in Puglia's agricultural tradition, boasting organically cultivated produce and unassuming guest rooms. Guests are treated to delightful dinners held around three times a week, featuring farm-fresh organic produce. Occasionally, these evenings showcase demonstrations of Pizzica, a traditional form of music and dance. The farm premises house goats, horses, and hens, providing visitors with a rustic and authentic countryside encounter.

While specific attractions around the Masseria aren't mentioned, its strategic location in the heart of Salento offers convenient access to both coasts and various points of interest in the area. Visitors can explore the diverse attractions this region has to offer during their stay at Masseria Sant'Angelo Agriturismo.

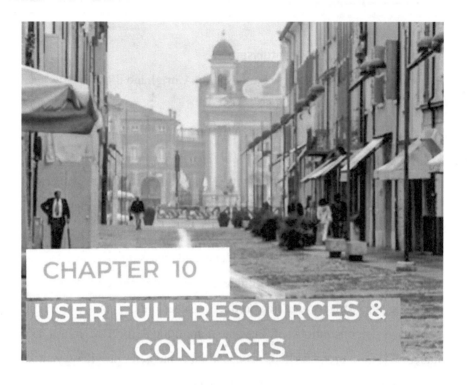

CHAPTER 10
USER FULL RESOURCES & CONTACTS

Puglia Fastival Not to Miss

Local Phrase

Tourist Information Centers

Emergency Contacts

CHAPTER 10

USER FULL RESOURCES & CONTACTS

Puglia Festival Not to Miss

Here are some of the festivals and events in Puglia; please note that this is just a handful of the hundreds of events in Puglia throughout the year. For more detailed information, it's recommended to ask at the local tourist office:

January-April: Il Carnevale di Putignano

Celebrated up to Shrove Tuesday, this carnival, one of Europe's oldest, fills Putignano with four vibrant parades, festive parties, and playful masquerades. Expect a mix of tradition and modernity with various events, including a mini-summer carnival in early July.

March-April: Easter Week

Across Puglia, Easter Week is marked by poignant processions and passion plays, evoking deep religious reflection and devotion, offering a profound experience of local traditions and faith.

First half of April: European Film Festival in Lecce

A six-day extravaganza showcasing a diverse range of European films, this festival in Lecce is a cinephile's delight, offering a glimpse into Europe's cinematic diversity.

Late April: Bari International Film Festival

A week-long celebration of global cinema, this festival in Bari features a broad spectrum of international films, making it a cultural treat for movie enthusiasts.

7th-9th May: La Festa di San Nicola in Bari

This three-day festivity attracts pilgrims worldwide to honour Saint Nicholas with vibrant celebrations and religious rituals, transforming Bari into a lively hub of reverence.

8th-10th May: La Festa di San Cataldo in Taranto

A tribute to the city's patron saint, San Cataldo, this three-day celebration in Taranto promises colourful processions and cultural fervour.

End of June: Danza delle Tarantole at Galatina

Embrace the traditional Italian folk dance, the Tarantella, during this lively celebration at Galatina, offering a vibrant spectacle of music and dance.

July: Fasano Music Festival

Fasano hosts a captivating music festival in July, featuring a diverse lineup of musical performances and creating an eclectic atmosphere for music lovers.

July: Otranto Jazz Festival

Set in the picturesque Otranto castle, this three-day Jazz festival in July delivers soulful melodies and dynamic performances, attracting music enthusiasts.

July: La Ghironda, Ostuni festival

Ostuni hosts a multicultural celebration embracing music and culture from five continents, offering a diverse showcase of global artistry.

Mid-July to early August: Festival della Valle d'Itria at Martina Franca

In Martina Franca, indulge in a classical music fiesta, including opera, during this festival that captivates with its musical elegance and grandeur.

August (2-3 weeks): La Notte della Taranta in Melpignano

Experience the largest Tarantella celebration across Salento with concerts, folk music, dancing, and vibrant festivities honouring this traditional Italian dance.

Mid-August: Festival of the Holy Martyrs in Otranto

Commemorating the 1480 massacre, this event in Otranto recalls the historical event with solemn ceremonies and cultural activities.

Late August: Festa di Sant'Oronzo in Lecce

Lecce honours its patron saint with a lively festival featuring musical performances, delectable local cuisines, and captivating fireworks.

Late September: Commemorations in San Giovanni Rotondo

Marking Padre Pio's passing, this event in San Giovanni Rotondo includes festivals at Monte Sant'Angelo, embracing religious traditions.

December: Christmas Festivities

Puglia rings in the holiday season with religious events and enchanting nativity scenes, providing a spiritual ambience amidst festive cheer.

Local Phrase

Greetings:

- Hello: "Ciao" or "Salve"
- Good morning: "Buongiorno"
- Good afternoon/evening: "Buonasera"
- Goodbye: "Arrivederci"
- Please: "Per favore"
- Thank you: "Grazie"
- Excuse me: "Scusi"

Transportation:

- Where is the bus/train station? - "Dov'è la stazione degli autobus/treni?"

- How much is a ticket to...? - "Quanto costa un biglietto per...?"
- I'd like a taxi, please - "Vorrei un taxi, per favore"
- Where is the nearest metro station? - "Dov'è la stazione della metropolitana più vicina?"
- How much is the fare?: Quanto costa la tariffa?

Security and Emergency:
- Help! - "Aiuto!"
- I need the police - "Ho bisogno della polizia"
- Where is the nearest hospital? - "Dov'è l'ospedale più vicino?"
- I've lost my bag - "Ho perso la mia borsa"

Hotel:
- I have a reservation - "Ho una prenotazione"
- Is breakfast included? - "La colazione è inclusa?"
- Can I have a wake-up call, please? - "Posso avere una sveglia, per favore?"

Restaurants:
- The menu, please: Il menu, per favore
- Table for two, please - "Un tavolo per due, per favore"
- I would like to order: Vorrei ordinare
- What do you recommend? - "Cosa consiglia?"
- The bill, please - "Il conto, per favore"

Time and Numbers:

- What time is it? - "Che ora è?"
- Today: Oggi
- Tomorrow: Domani
- Days: Monday (lunedì), Tuesday (martedì), Wednesday (mercoledì), Thursday (giovedì), Friday (venerdì), Saturday (sabato), Sunday (domenica)

Numbers: 1 (uno), 2 (due), 3 (tre), 4 (quattro), 5 (cinque), 6 (sei), 7 (sette), 8 (otto), 9 (nove), 10 (dieci)

Shopping:

- How much does this cost? - "Quanto costa questo?"
- Can I pay by card? - "Posso pagare con la carta?"

Sightseeing:

- Where is the museum?: Dov'è il museo?
- Can you recommend a good place to visit?: Puoi consigliare un buon posto da visitare?
- Where is the nearest tourist attraction? - "Dov'è la attrazione turistica più vicina?"
- Could you take a photo, please? - "Potrebbe scattare una foto, per favore?"
- I'm lost - "Mi sono perso/a"

Asking for Help

- Can you help me, please?: Puoi **aiutarmi**, per favore?
- I am lost: Sono perso
- I need a doctor: Ho bisogno di **un dottore**
- Where is the hospital?: Dov'è l'**ospedale**?

Tourist Information Centers

To facilitate a seamless and enjoyable experience for travelers, numerous Tourist Information Centers are strategically located across the region. These centers serve as valuable resources, offering a wealth of information, guidance, and assistance for visitors exploring Puglia's diverse landscapes, cultural heritage, and vibrant communities.

Bari

- Bari Tourist Information Office
- Location: Piazza Moro, 4, 70122 Bari BA
- Contact: +39 080 524 2424

This centrally located office provides comprehensive information about Bari's attractions, accommodations, transport, and local events. Knowledgeable staff offer guidance in multiple languages.

Brindisi

- Brindisi Tourist Information Office
- Location: Lungomare Regina Margherita, 1, 72100 Brindisi BR
- Contact: +39 0831 522889

Situated along the picturesque waterfront, this office caters to tourists seeking information about Brindisi's historical sites, ferry services, local festivals, and accommodations.

Lecce

- Lecce Tourist Information Center
- Location: Via degli Ammirati, 11, 73100 Lecce LE
- Contact: +39 0832 244111

Positioned within the historic district, this center provides insights into Lecce's renowned baroque architecture, cultural events, guided tours, and dining recommendations.

Taranto

Taranto Tourist Information Office

- Location: Viale Virgilio, 35, 74121 Taranto TA
- Contact: +39 099 470 4490

Catering to visitors exploring Taranto's ancient history, this center offers details on archeological sites, local traditions, museum schedules, and accommodation options.

Foggia

Foggia Tourist Information Office

- Location: Piazza Umberto Giordano, 1, 71100 Foggia FG
- Contact: +39 0881 780231

Situated in the heart of Foggia, this center assists travelers with information on nearby national parks, transportation links, and rural experiences in the Gargano area.

Useful Resources

Puglia Tourism Board (APT Puglia)

Website: www.viaggiareinpuglia.it

Services: A comprehensive online platform offering detailed insights into Puglia's destinations, accommodations, itineraries, events, and suggested activities.

Here are the contact details for some of the I.A.T. centers in Puglia:

- Alberobello: Via Monte Nero, 3. Tel: +39 080 4322060
- Andria: Piazza Catuma, Tel: +39 0883 290293
- Barletta: Corso Garibaldi 208, Tel: +39 0883 53155

Emergency Contacts

Medical Emergencies

In the event of a medical emergency, it's crucial to seek immediate assistance. Hospitals and emergency services are available throughout Puglia.

Emergency Medical Services (Ambulance)

Dial: 112 or 118

Services: Trained medical professionals respond to urgent medical situations. Call for immediate medical attention, available 24/7.

Hospitals in Puglia

- Bari: Policlinico di Bari - +39 080 5592111
- Brindisi: Ospedale Perrino - +39 0831 541111
- Lecce: Vito Fazzi Hospital - +39 0832 661111
- Taranto: Azienda Ospedaliera SS. Annunziata - +39 099 4581111
- Foggia: Ospedale Riuniti di Foggia - +39 0881 730111

Police and Law Enforcement

In case of emergencies requiring police intervention or reporting a crime:

Emergency Police Services

Dial: 112

Services: Contact the police for immediate assistance or to report criminal activities. Available 24/7.

Fire and Rescue Services

For fire emergencies or accidents requiring rescue services:

Fire Department (Vigili del Fuoco)

Dial: 115

Services: Contact the fire department in case of fires, accidents, or other emergencies requiring rescue services.

Emergency Assistance for Tourists

For specific assistance or guidance catering to tourists in Puglia:

Tourist Police

Location: Contact the local police station or Carabinieri for tourist-related issues or guidance.

Italian Tourist Helpline

Dial: 039 06 491770

Services: Provides information and assistance in various languages for tourists in Italy.

Useful Resources

Emergency Numbers Overview

Website: European Emergency Number Association (EENA)

Services: Offers a comprehensive overview of emergency numbers across Europe, including Italy's emergency contact details.

Important Tips

Language Barrier: In emergencies, English may only sometimes be widely spoken. Try to communicate in basic Italian phrases or have a translation app available.

Identification and Documentation: Always carry identification, insurance details, and relevant documents for medical emergencies.

CONCLUSION

Thank you for choosing our Puglia travel guide, a gateway to the captivating region of Italy. As you journey through Puglia's diverse landscapes, timeless culture, and rich heritage, may this guide be your trusted companion, unveiling hidden gems and facilitating unforgettable experiences.

In bidding you farewell from the sun-soaked coastlines, enchanting villages, and vibrant cities of Puglia, we extend our heartfelt wishes. May the warmth of Salento's hospitality, the allure of Valle d'Itria's trulli, and the essence of Puglia's culinary delights linger in your memories. Here's to unforgettable adventures and the joy of discovering the beauty woven into the fabric of Puglia. Safe travels and arrivederci from this captivating corner of Italy!

THANK YOU

> Thank you for taking the time to read my book. I hope it provided you with some enlightenment, entertainment, or both. If you enjoyed it, I would be most grateful if you could leave a review on Amazon. Reviews are invaluable to authors, as they help spread the word about the book and give potential readers an idea of what to expect.
>
> Your honest opinion, even if it's not glowing, would be greatly appreciated and immensely helpful.
>
> Thank you for your consideration.

• • •

Happy holidays

TRAVEL *journal*

Location	Date

Where I Stayed

How I Travelled

TODAY'S BEST MOMENT

What I Did Today

What I Saw Today

NOTE

Location	Date

Where I Stayed

How I Travelled

TODAY'S BEST MOMENT

What I Did Today

What I Saw Today

Date _____

NOTE

Location	Date

Where I Stayed

How I Travelled

TODAY'S BEST MOMENT

What I Did Today *What I Saw Today*

NOTE

Location   Date

Where I Stayed

How I Travelled

TODAY'S BEST MOMENT

What I Did Today   *What I Saw Today*

Date

NOTE

Location	Date

Where I Stayed

How I Travelled

TODAY'S BEST MOMENT

What I Did Today

What I Saw Today

NOTE

| Location | Date |

Where I Stayed

How I Travelled

TODAY'S BEST MOMENT

| What I Did Today | What I Saw Today |

Date

NOTE

Location	Date

Where I Stayed

How I Travelled

TODAY'S BEST MOMENT

What I Did Today

What I Saw Today

Date _____

NOTE